Programming
Pearls

Programming Pearls

JON BENTLEY

AT&T Bell Laboratories
Murray Hill, New Jersey

▲▲▼

ADDISON-WESLEY PUBLISHING COMPANY

Reading, Massachusetts • Menlo Park, California
Don Mills, Ontario • Wokingham, England • Amsterdam
Sydney • Singapore • Tokyo • Mexico City
Bogotá • Santiago • San Juan

Mark S. Dalton/Publisher
James T. DeWolf/Sponsoring Editor

Hugh Crawford/Manufacturing Supervisor
Karen Guardino/Managing Editor
Laura Skinger/Production Supervisor

Library of Congress Cataloging-in-Publication Data

Bentley, Jon Louis.
  Programming pearls.

  Includes bibliographies and index.
  1. Electronic digital computers—Programming—
Addresses, essays, lectures.   I. Title.
QA76.6.B453 1986   005   85-20088
ISBN 0-201-10331-1

Reprinted with corrections April, 1986

This book was typeset in Times Roman and Courier by the author, using a Mergenthaler Linotron 202 phototypesetter driven by a VAX-11/750 running the 8th Edition of the 'JNIX operating system.

Cray-1 is a trademark of Cray Research, Inc. DEC, PDP and VAX are trademarks of Digital Equipment Corporation. TRS-80 is a trademark of Tandy Corporation. UNIX is a trademark of AT&T Bell Laboratories.

BCDEFGHIJ-DO-89876

PREFACE

Computer programming has many faces. Fred Brooks paints the big picture in his *Mythical Man Month*; his essays underscore the crucial role of management in large software projects. At a finer grain, Kernighan and Plauger teach good "programming-in-the-small" in their *Elements of Programming Style*. The topics in those books are the key to good software and the hallmark of the professional programmer. Unfortunately, though, the workmanlike application of those sound engineering principles isn't always thrilling — until the software is completed on time and works without surprise.

The essays in this book are about a more glamorous aspect of the profession: programming pearls whose origins lie beyond solid engineering, in the realm of insight and creativity. Just as natural pearls grow from grains of sand that have irritated oysters, these programming pearls have grown from real problems that have irritated real programmers. The programs are fun, and they teach important programming techniques and fundamental design principles.

These essays are selected from my "Programming Pearls" column in *Communications of the Association for Computing Machinery*; the publication history can be found in the introductions to Parts I, II and III. The versions in this book have been substantially revised since they appeared in *CACM*: new sections have been added, old sections underwent hundreds of little improvements, and ties between columns have been strengthened (for more details, peek ahead to the Epilog). The only background the columns assume is programming experience in a high-level language. More advanced techniques (such as recursion) show up every now and then, but the reader unfamiliar with such topics may skip to the next section with impunity.

Although each column can be read by itself, there is a logical grouping to the complete set. Columns 1 through 4 are Part I of the book. They review programming fundamentals: problem definition, algorithms, data structures, and program verification. Columns 5 through 9 are Part II. They are built around the theme of efficiency, which is sometimes important in itself and is always a fine springboard into interesting programming problems. The columns in Part III apply the techniques of the earlier columns to several substantial problems.

One hint about reading the columns: don't go too fast. Read them well, one per sitting. Try the problems as they are posed — some of them look easy until you've butted your head against them for an hour or two. Afterwards, work hard on the problems at the end: most of what you learn from this book will come out the end of your pencil as you scribble down your solutions. If possible, discuss your ideas with friends and colleagues before peeking at the hints and solutions in the back of the book. The further reading at the end of each chapter isn't intended as a scholarly reference list; I've recommended some good books that are an important part of my personal library.

This book is written for programmers. I hope that the problems, hints, solutions, and further reading make it useful for individual programmers, be they professionals or hobbyists. I have used drafts in undergraduate classes on "Applied Algorithm Design" and "Software Engineering"; supplemental educational materials are available from the publisher. The catalog of algorithms in the Appendix is a handy reference for practicing programmers, and also shows how the book can be integrated into classes on algorithms and data structures.

I am grateful for much support from many people. The idea for a *Communications of the ACM* column was originally conceived by Peter Denning and Stuart Lynn. Peter worked diligently within ACM to make the column possible and recruited me for the job. ACM Headquarters staff, particularly Roz Steier and Nancy Adriance, have been very supportive as these columns were published in their original form. I am especially indebted to the ACM for encouraging publication of the columns in their present form, and to the many *CACM* readers who made this expanded version necessary and possible by their comments on the original columns.

Al Aho, Peter Denning, Mike Garey, David Johnson, Brian Kernighan, John Linderman, Doug McIlroy and Don Stanat have all read each column with great care, often under extreme time pressure. I am also grateful for the particularly helpful comments of Henry Baird, Marilyn Bentley, Bill Cleveland, David Gries, Eric Grosse, Lynn Jelinski, Steve Johnson, Bob Melville, Bob Martin, Arno Penzias, Chris Van Wyk, Vic Vyssotsky and Pamela Zave. Al Aho, Andrew Hume, Brian Kernighan, Ravi Sethi, Laura Skinger and Bjarne Stroustrup provided invaluable help in bookmaking, and West Point cadets in EF 485 field tested the penultimate draft of the manuscript. Thanks, all.

Murray Hill, New Jersey   J. B.

CONTENTS

PART I: **PRELIMINARIES**

These four columns review the basics of programming. Column 1 is the history of a single problem. A combination of careful problem definition and straightforward programming techniques led to an elegant solution. The case illustrates the central theme of this book: thinking hard about a real programming problem can be fun and can also lead to practical benefits.

Column 2 examines three problems, with an emphasis on how algorithmic insights can yield simple programs. Column 3 surveys the crucial role that data structures play in program design.

Column 4 introduces program verification and the role it can play as code is written. Verification techniques are used extensively in Columns 8, 10 and 12.

These were the first columns published in the "Programming Pearls" section of *Communications of the ACM*. Column 1 appeared in the August 1983 issue, Column 2 in September, Column 3 in October, and Column 4 in December.

COLUMN 1: **CRACKING THE OYSTER**

The programmer's question was simple: "How do I sort on disk?" Before I tell you how I made my first mistake, let me give you a chance to do better than I did. What would you have said?

1.1 A Friendly Conversation

My mistake was to answer his question. I gave him a thumbnail sketch on how to sort on disk. My suggestion that he dig into Knuth's classic *Sorting and Searching* met with less than enthusiasm — he was more concerned about solving the problem than with furthering his education. I then told him about the disk sorting program in Chapter 4 of Kernighan and Plauger's *Software Tools*. Their program consists of about two hundred lines of Ratfor code in twelve procedures; translating that into several hundred lines of FORTRAN and testing the code would have taken about a week.

I thought that I had solved his problem, but his hesitation led me back to the right track. The conversation then went something like this, with my questions in *italics*.

Why do you want to write a sort routine at all? Why not use the system sort?

I need the sort in the middle of a large system, and the operating system doesn't provide a way to escape from a user program to a system routine.

What exactly are you sorting? How many records are in the file? What is the format of each record?

The file contains at most 27,000 records; each record is a 16-bit integer.

Wait a minute. If the file is that small, why bother going to disk at all? Why not just sort it in main memory?

Although the machine has half a megabyte of main memory, this routine is part of a big program. I expect that I'll have only about a thousand 16-bit words free at that point.

Is there anything else you can tell me about the records?

3

Each one is an integer in the range 1..27,000, and no integer can appear more than once.

The context makes the problem clearer. The system was used for political redistricting (automated gerrymandering), and the numbers to be sorted were indices of precincts that make up a political district. Each precinct within a state had a unique number from 1 to 27,000 (the number of precincts in the largest state), and it was illegal to include the same precinct twice in one district. The desired output was a list of the precinct numbers in a district, sorted in numeric order. The context also defines the performance requirements: since the user interrupted the design session roughly once an hour to invoke the sort and could do nothing until it was completed, the sort couldn't take more than a few minutes, while a few seconds was a more desirable run time.

1.2 Precise Problem Statement

To the programmer these requirements added up to "How do I sort on disk?" Before we attack the problem, let's arrange the facts in a less biased and more useful form.

Input: A file containing at most 27,000 integers in the range 1..27,000. It is a fatal error condition if any integer occurs twice in the input. No other data is associated with the integer.

Output: A sorted list in increasing order of the input integers.

Constraints: At most (roughly) one thousand 16-bit words of storage are available in main memory; disk buffers in main memory and ample disk storage are available. The run time can be at most several minutes; a run time of ten seconds need not be decreased.

Think again for a minute; how would you advise the programmer now?

1.3 Program Design

The obvious program uses Kernighan and Plauger's general disk sorting program as a base but trims it to exploit the fact that we are sorting integers. That reduces their 200 lines of code by a few dozen lines, and also makes it run faster. It would still take quite a while to get the code up and running.

A second solution makes even more use of the particular nature of this sorting problem; its main loop makes 27 passes over the input file. On the first pass it reads into memory any integer between 1 and 1000, sorts the (at most) 1000 integers and writes them to the output file. The second pass sorts the integers from 1001 to 2000, and so on to the twenty-seventh pass, which sorts 26,001 to 27,000. Kernighan and Plauger's Quicksort would be quite efficient for the in-core sorts, and it requires only about forty lines of Ratfor code (we'll see several sorts in Columns 10 and 12). The entire program could therefore be implemented in about eighty lines of FORTRAN. It also has the desirable property that we no longer have to worry about using intermediate disk files; unfortunately, for that benefit we pay the price of reading the entire input file 27 times.

A merge sort program reads the file once from the input, sorts it with the aid of work files that are read and written many times, and then writes it once.

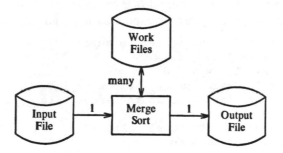

The 27-pass algorithm reads the input file many times and writes the output just once, using no intermediate files.

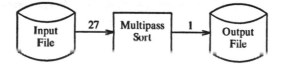

We would prefer the following scheme, which combines the advantages of the previous two. It reads the input just once, and uses no intermediate files.

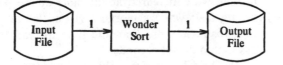

We can do this only if we represent all the integers in the input file in the roughly one thousand available words of main memory. Thus the problem boils down to whether we can represent the 27,000 distinct integers in *about* 16,000 available bits. Think for a minute about an appropriate representation.

1.4 Implementation Sketch

Viewed in this light, the *bitmap* or *bit vector* representation of a set screams out to be used. We'll represent the file by a string of 27,000 bits in which the Ith bit is on if and only if the integer I is in the file. (The programmer found 11,000 spare bits; Problem 1 investigates the case that 16,000 is a firm limit.) This representation uses three attributes of this problem not usually found in sorting problems: the input is from a small range, it contains no duplicates, and no data is associated with each record beyond the single integer.

Given the bitmap data structure to represent the set of integers in the file, the program can be written in three natural phases. The first phase initializes the set to empty by turning off all bits. The second phase builds the set by reading each integer in the file and turning on the appropriate bit. The third phase produces the sorted output file by inspecting each bit and writing out the appropriate integer if the bit is one. If N is the number of bits in the vector (in this case 27,000), the program can be expressed in pseudocode as:

```
/* Phase 1: Initialize set to empty */
    for I := 1 to N do
        Bit[I] := 0
/* Phase 2: Insert present elements into the set */
    for each integer I in the input file
        Bit[I] := 1
/* Phase 3: Output sorted files */
    for I := 1 to N do
        if Bit[I] = 1 then
            write I on the output file
```

This sketch was sufficient for the programmer to solve his problem. Some of the implementation details he faced are described in Problems 1, 2 and 6.

1.5 Principles

The programmer told me about his problem in a phone call; it took us about fifteen minutes to get to the real problem and find the bitmap solution. It took him a couple of hours to implement the program in a few dozen lines of FORTRAN; that compares quite nicely with the hundreds of lines of code and the week of programming time we had feared at the start of the phone call. And the program was lightning fast: while a merge sort on disk might take several minutes, this program takes little more than the time to read the input and to write the output — less than a dozen seconds.

Those facts contain the first lesson from this case study: careful analysis of a small problem can sometimes yield tremendous practical benefits. In this case a few minutes of careful study led to an order of magnitude reduction in code length, programmer time, and run time. General Chuck Yeager (the first person to fly faster than sound) praised an airplane's engine system with the words "simple, few parts, easy to maintain, very strong"; this program shares those attributes. The program's specialized structure, however, would be hard to modify if certain dimensions of the specifications were changed. In addition to the advertising for clever programming, this case illustrates the following general principles.

The Right Problem. Defining the problem was about ninety percent of this battle — I'm glad that the programmer didn't settle for the first program I described. Problems 9 and 10 have elegant solutions once you pose the right problem; think hard about them before looking at the hints and solutions.

The Bitmap Data Structure. This data structure represents a dense set over a finite domain when each element occurs at most once and there is no other data associated with the element. Even if these conditions aren't satisfied (when there are multiple elements or extra data), a key from a finite domain can be used as an index into a table with more complicated entries.

Multiple-Pass Algorithms. These algorithms make several passes over their input data, accomplishing a little bit more each time. We saw a 27-pass algorithm earlier; Problem 1 encourages you to develop a two-pass algorithm.

A Time-Space Tradeoff and One That Isn't. Programming folklore and theory abound with time-space tradeoffs: by using more time, a program can run in less space. The two-pass algorithm in Solution 1, for instance, doubles a program's run time to halve its space. It has been my experience more frequently, though, that reducing a program's space requirements also reduces its run time.† The space-efficient structure of bitmaps dramatically reduced the run time of sorting. There were two reasons that the reduction in space led to a reduction in time: less data to process means less time to process it, and keeping data in main memory rather than on disk avoids the overhead of disk accesses. Of course, the mutual improvement was possible only because the original design was far from optimal.

A Simple Design. Antoine de Saint-Exupéry, the French writer and aircraft designer, said that "a designer knows he has arrived at perfection not when there is no longer anything to add, but when there is no longer anything to take away". More programmers should judge their work by this criterion. Simple programs are usually more reliable, secure, robust and efficient than their complex cousins, and a lot easier to build and to maintain.

Stages of Program Design. This case illustrates the design process that is described in detail in Section 11.4.

1.6 Problems

Hints for and solutions to selected problems can be found in sections at the back of the book.

1. The programmer said that he had about a thousand words of free storage, but the code we sketched uses 27,000/16=1688 words. He was able to scrounge the extra space without much trouble. If the 1000 words of space had been a hard and fast boundary, what would you have recommended? What is the run time of your algorithm?

---

† Tradeoffs are common to all engineering disciplines; automobile designers, for instance, usually trade reduced mileage for better performance by adding heavy components. Mutual improvements are preferred, though. A review of the economy car I drive observes that "the weight saving on the car's basic structure translates into further weight reductions in the various chassis components — and even the elimination of the need for some, such as power steering".

2. One barrier between the code sketch and a complete FORTRAN program is the implementation of bitmaps. While this would be trivial in programming languages that support bitmaps as a primitive data type, FORTRAN programmers must usually implement them using other operations. Suppose that the FORTRAN dialect provided bitwise logical operations on words (such as shifting, ANDing and ORing); how would you advise the programmer to implement bit vectors? How could you implement bitmaps if those logical operations were not available? How would you implement this algorithm in COBOL? In Pascal?

3. Run-time efficiency was an important part of the design goal, and the resulting program was efficient enough. Implement the bitmap program on your system and measure its run time; how does it compare to the system sort on the same file?

4. If you take Problem 3 seriously, you will face the problem of generating K integers between 1 and 27,000 without duplicates. The simplest approach uses the first K positive integers. This extreme data set won't alter the run time of the bitmap method by much, but it might lead to a system sort that is much faster than on typical data. How could you generate a file of K unique random integers between 1 and N in random order? Strive for a short program that is also efficient.

5. What would you recommend to the programmer if, instead of saying that each integer could appear at most once, he told you that each integer could appear at most ten times? How would your solution change as a function of the amount of available storage?

6. [R. Weil] The program as sketched has several flaws. The first is that it assumes that no integer appears twice in the input. What happens if one does show up more than once? How could the program be modified to call an error routine in that case? What happens when an input integer is less than one or greater than N? What should a program do under those circumstances? Describe small data sets that test the program, including its proper handling of these and other ill-behaved cases.

7. In a college registration system a programmer needed a data structure to count the seats available in various courses. Each of 6,000 courses had a unique four-digit identification number (from 0000 to 9999) and a three-digit seat count (from 000 to 999). After building the data structure from a file of course numbers and seat counts, the program was to process a tape of about 80,000 requests for courses.

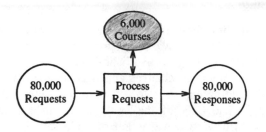

Each request for a valid course number was either denied (if the seat count was zero) or approved (in which case the seat count was decremented by one); requests for invalid course numbers were marked as such and ignored. After allocating object code space, buffers, and the like, the system had about 30 kilobytes of main memory available to the user. In his first design of a COBOL program the programmer considered representing each course as a seven-byte disk record (four for course number and three for seat count); the disk operations would have made this structure prohibitively expensive. Is there a better way to organize the course information?

8. One problem with trading more space to use less time is that initializing the space can itself take a great deal of time. Show how to circumvent this problem by designing a technique to initialize an entry of a vector to zero the first time it is accessed. Your scheme should use constant time for initialization and for each vector access; you may use extra space proportional to the size of the vector. Because this method reduces initialization time by using even more space, it should be considered only when space is cheap, time is dear and the vector is sparse. (This problem is from Exercise 2.12 of Aho, Hopcroft and Ullman's *Design and Analysis of Computer Algorithms*, published by Addison-Wesley in 1974.)

9. Department stores in a certain large chain allow customers to order catalog items over the telephone, which they pick up a few days later. The store's database uses the customer's telephone number as the primary key for retrieval (customers know their phone numbers and the keys are close to unique). How would you organize the database to allow orders to be inserted and retrieved efficiently?

10. In 1981 Lockheed engineers had to transmit daily about a dozen drawings from a Computer Aided Design (CAD) system in their Sunnyvale, California, plant to a test station in Santa Cruz. Although the facilities were just 25 miles apart, an automobile courier service took over an hour (due to traffic jams and mountain roads) and cost a hundred dollars per day. Propose alternative data transmission schemes and estimate their cost.

1.7 Further Reading

On the way to building their *Software Tools*, Kernighan and Plauger solve many small (but difficult and rewarding) programming problems. The book was originally published in 1976 by Addison-Wesley; a later version with the same theme but many important changes appeared in 1981 as *Software Tools in Pascal*. Their tool-building approach to software can change the way you think about programming. The bulk of the book shows programming the way it should be: the straightforward construction of code that is easy to use and to maintain.

Often, though, the book rises above mere good practice to subtle solutions to hard problems. The index entries of "algorithms" and "data structures" point to many of these pearls. Unfortunately, subtle ideas are often presented in such a straightforward way that the poor reader may think they're easy. When you read this important book, be sure to take time to appreciate those pearls: they're beautiful, and they're based on powerful techniques.

In the case study described in this column, the programmer's main problem was not so much technical as psychological: he couldn't make progress because he was trying to solve the wrong problem. We finally solved his problem by breaking through his conceptual block and solving an easier problem. *Conceptual Blockbusting* by James L. Adams (Second Edition published by Norton in 1979) studies this kind of leap and is generally a pleasant prod towards more creative thinking. Although it was not written with programmers in mind, many of its lessons are particularly appropriate for programming problems. Adams defines conceptual blocks as "mental walls that block the problem-solver from correctly perceiving a problem or conceiving its solution"; Problems 9 and 10 encourage you to bust some.

COLUMN 2: **AHA! ALGORITHMS**

The study of algorithms offers much to the practicing programmer. A course on the subject equips students with algorithms for important tasks and design techniques for attacking new problems. We'll see in later columns how advanced algorithmic tools sometimes have a substantial impact on software systems, both in reduced development time and faster execution speed.

As crucial as those sophisticated ideas are, algorithms have a more important impact at a more common level of programming. In his book *Aha! Insight* (from which I shamelessly stole my title), Martin Gardner describes the contribution I have in mind: "A problem that seems difficult may have a simple, unexpected solution." Unlike the advanced methods, the *aha!* insights of algorithms don't come only after extensive study; they're available to any programmer willing to think seriously before, during, and after coding.

2.1 Three Problems

Enough generalities. This column is built around three little problems; try them before you read on.

A. Given a tape that contains at most one million twenty-bit integers in random order, find a twenty-bit integer that isn't on the tape (and there must be at least one missing — why?). How would you solve this problem with ample quantities of main memory? How would you solve it if you had several tape drives but only a few dozen words of main memory?

B. Rotate a one-dimensional array of N elements left by I positions. For instance, with $N=8$ and $I=3$, the vector *ABCDEFGH* is rotated to *DEFGHABC*. Simple code uses an N-element intermediate vector to do the job in N steps. Can you rotate the vector in time proportional to N using only a few extra words of storage?

C. Given a dictionary of English words, find all sets of anagrams. For instance, "pots", "stop" and "tops" are all anagrams of one another because each can be formed by permuting the letters of the others.

11

Binary Search

I'm thinking of an integer between 1 and 100; you guess it. Fifty? Too low. Seventy-five? Too high. And so the game goes, until you guess my number. If my integer is originally between 1 and N, then you can guess it in $\log_2 N$ guesses. If N is a thousand, ten guesses will do, and if N is a million, you'll need at most twenty.

This example illustrates a technique that solves a multitude of programming problems: *binary search*. We initially know that an object is within a given range, and a probe operation tells us whether the object is below, at, or above a given position. Binary search locates the object by repeatedly probing the middle of the current range. If the probe doesn't find the object, then we halve the current range and continue. We stop when we find what we're looking for or when the range becomes empty.

The most common application of binary search in programming is to search for an element in a sorted array. When looking for the entry 50, the algorithm makes the following probes.

26	26	31	31	32	38	38	41	43	46	50	53	58	59	79	97

A binary search program is notoriously hard to get right; we'll study the code in detail in Column 4.

Sequential search uses about $N/2$ comparisons on the average to search a table of N elements, while binary search never uses more than about $\log_2 N$ comparisons. That can make a big difference in system performance; this typical anecdote is from the July 1984 *Communications of the ACM* case study that describes "The TWA Reservation System".

> We had one program that was doing a linear search through a very large piece of core almost 100 times a second. As the network grew, the average CPU time per message was up 0.3 milliseconds, which is a huge jump for us. We traced the problem to the linear search, changed the application program to use a binary search, and the problem went away.

But the story of binary search doesn't end with rapidly searching sorted arrays. Roy Weil of Michael Baker Jr., Inc., applied the technique in cleaning a deck of about a thousand punched cards that contained a single bad card. Unfortunately, the bad card wasn't known by sight; it could be identified only by running a subset of the cards through a program and seeing a wildly erroneous answer, which took several minutes. His predecessors at debugging tried to spot it by running a few cards at a time through the program, and they were making progress towards a solution at a snail's pace. How did Weil find the culprit in just ten runs of the program?

With this warmup, we can tackle Problem A. Given a tape that contains at most one million twenty-bit integers in random order, we are to find one twenty-bit integer not on the tape. (There must be at least one missing, because there are 2^{20} or 1,048,576 such integers.) With ample main memory, we could use the bit-vector technique from Column 1 and dedicate 131,072 8-bit bytes to a bitmap representing the integers seen so far. The problem, however, also asks how we can find the missing integer if we have only a few dozen words of main memory and several extra tape drives. To set this up as a binary search we have to define a range, a representation for the elements within the range, and a probing method to determine which half of a range holds the missing integer. How can we do this?

We'll use as the range a sequence of integers known to contain at least one missing element, and we'll represent the range by a tape containing all the integers in it. The insight is that we can probe a range by counting the elements above and below its midpoint: either the upper or the lower range has at most half the elements in the total range. Because the total range has a missing element, the lesser half must also have a missing element. These are most of the ingredients of a binary search algorithm for the problem; try putting them together yourself before you peek at the solutions to see how Ed Reingold did it.

These uses of binary search just scratch the surface of its applications in programming. A root finder uses binary search to solve a single-variable equation by successively halving an interval; numerical analysts call this the bisection method. When the selection algorithm in Solution 10.9 partitions around a random element and then calls itself recursively on all elements on one side of that element, it is using a "randomized" binary search. Other uses of binary search include tree data structures, data processing algorithms that run on card sorters (which use the corresponding decimal search), and program debugging (when a program dies a silent death, where do you place print commands to home in on the guilty statement?). In each of these examples, thinking of the program as a few embellishments on top of the basic binary search algorithm can give the programmer that all-powerful *aha!*

2.3 The Power of Primitives

Binary search is a solution that looks for problems; we'll now study a problem that has several solutions. Problem B is to rotate the N-element vector X left by I positions in time proportional to N and with just a few words of extra space. This problem arises in applications in various guises: mathematical languages such as APL provide rotation as a primitive operation on vectors. On pages 194-195 of their *Software Tools in Pascal*, Kernighan and Plauger use a rotation routine in their implementation of a text editor. The time and space constraints are important in both applications.

One might try to solve the problem by copying the first I elements of X to a temporary vector, moving the remaining $N-I$ elements left I places, and then copying the first I from the temporary vector back to the last positions in X. However, the I extra words of space used by this scheme make it too space-expensive. For a different approach, we could define a subroutine to rotate X left one position (in time proportional to N) and call it I times, but that is too time-expensive.

To solve the problem within the resource bounds will apparently require a more complicated program. One successful approach is just a delicate juggling act: move $X[1]$ to the temporary T, and then move $X[I+1]$ to $X[1]$, $X[2I+1]$ to $X[I+1]$, and so on (taking all indices into X modulo N), until we come back to taking an element from $X[1]$, at which point we instead take the element from T and stop the process. When I is 3 and N is 12, that phase moves the elements in this order.

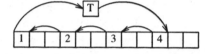

If that process didn't move all the elements, then we start over at $X[2]$, and continue until we move all the elements. Problem 3 challenges you to reduce this idea to code; be careful.

A different algorithm results from a different view of the problem: rotating the vector X is really just swapping the two segments of the vector AB to be the vector BA, where A represents the first I elements of X. Suppose A is shorter than B. Divide B into B_L and B_R so that B_R is the same length as A. Swap A and B_R to transform AB_LB_R into B_RB_LA. The sequence A is in its final place, so we can focus on swapping the two parts of B. Since this new problem has the same form as the original, we can solve it recursively. This algorithm can lead to an elegant program (Solution 3 describes an eight-line iterative solution due to Gries and Mills), but it requires delicate code and some thought to see that it is efficient enough.

The problem looks hard until you finally have the *aha!* insight: let's view the problem as transforming the array AB into the array BA, but let's also assume we have a subroutine that reverses the elements in a specified portion of the array. Starting with AB, we reverse A to get A^RB, reverse B to get A^RB^R, and then reverse the whole thing to get $(A^RB^R)^R$, which is exactly BA. This results in the following code for rotation; the comments show the results when $ABCDEFGH$ is rotated left three elements.

```
Reverse(1,I)            /* CBADEFGH */
Reverse(I+1,N)          /* CBAHGFED */
Reverse(1,N)            /* DEFGHABC */
```

This hand-waving example of rotating a ten-element array up five positions is due to Doug McIlroy; start with your palms towards you, left over right.

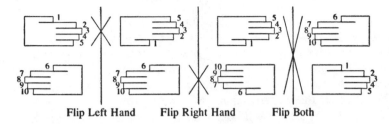

Flip Left Hand   Flip Right Hand   Flip Both

The reversal code is time- and space-efficient, and is so short and simple that it's pretty hard to get wrong. It is exactly the code that Kernighan and Plauger use in the text editor in their book. Brian Kernighan reports that this code ran correctly the first time it was executed, while their previous code for a similar task based on linked lists contained several bugs. This code is used in several text editors, including the UNIX system's ed editor with which I originally typed this column. Ken Thompson wrote the editor and the reversal code in 1971, and claims that it was part of the folklore even then.

2.4 Getting It Together: Sorting

Let's turn now to Problem C. Given a dictionary of English words (one word per input line in lower case letters), we must find all anagram classes. There are several good reasons for studying this problem. The first is technical: the solution is a nice combination of getting the right viewpoint and then using the right tools. The second reason is more compelling: wouldn't you hate to be the only person at a party who didn't know that "deposit", "dopiest", "posited" and "topside" are anagrams? And if those aren't enough, Problem 6 describes a similar problem in an application.

There are a number of surprisingly ineffective and complicated ways to solve this problem. Any method that considers all permutations of letters for a word is doomed to failure. The word "microphotographic" (an anagram of "photomicrographic") has 17! permutations, and a few multiplications showed that $17! \approx 3 \times 10^{14}$. Even assuming the blazing speed of one microsecond per permutation, this will take 3×10^8 seconds. The rule of thumb that "π seconds is a nanocentury" is true to within half a percent (there are roughly 3.155×10^9 seconds in a century), so the 3×10^8 seconds are almost a decade. And any method that compares all pairs of words is doomed to at least an overnight run on my machine — there are over seventy thousand words in the dictionary I used, and even a simple anagram comparison on my machine takes a couple dozen microseconds, so the total time is roughly

70,000 words × 70,000 comparisons/word × 25 microseconds/comparison

$$= 4900 \times 25 \times 10^6 \text{ microseconds} = 25 \times 4900 \text{ seconds} \approx 1.4 \text{ days}$$

Can you find a way to avoid both the above pitfalls?

The *aha!* insight is to sign each word in the dictionary so that words in the same anagram class have the same signature, and then bring together words with the same signatures. This reduces the original anagram problem to two subproblems: selecting a signature and collecting words with the same signature. Think about these problems before reading further.

For the first problem we'll use a signature based on sorting†: order the letters within the word alphabetically. The signature of "deposit" is "deiopst", which is also the signature of "dopiest" and any other word in that class. And that solves the second problem: sort the words in the order of their signatures. The best description I have heard of this algorithm is Tom Cargill's hand waving: sort this way (with a horizontal wave of the hand) then that way (a vertical wave). Section 2.8 describes an implementation of this algorithm.

2.5 Principles

Sorting. The most obvious use of sorting is to produce sorted output, either as part of the system specification or as preparation for another program (perhaps one that uses binary search). But in the anagram example, the ordering was not of interest; we sorted to bring together equal elements (in this case signatures). Those signatures are yet another application of sorting: ordering the letters within a word provides a *canonical form* for the words within an anagram class. By placing extra keys on each record and sorting by those keys, a sort routine can be used as a workhorse for rearranging data; this is especially powerful when dealing with large quantities of data on magnetic tapes — see Exercises 5-8 through 5-24 of Knuth's *Sorting and Searching*. We'll return to the subject of sorting several times in Part III.

Binary Search. The algorithm for looking up an element in a sorted table is remarkably efficient and can be used in main memory or on disk; its only drawback is that the entire table must be known and sorted in advance. The strategy underlying this simple algorithm is used in many other applications.

Signatures. When an equivalence relation defines classes, it is helpful to define a signature such that every item in a class has the same signature and no other item does. Sorting the letters within a word yields one signature for an anagram class; other signatures are given by sorting and then representing duplicates by a count (so the signature of "mississippi" might be "i4m1p2s4"

---

† This anagram algorithm has been independently discovered by many people, dating at least as far back as the mid-1960's. For further reading on anagrams and similar word problems, see A. K. Dewdney's "Computer Recreations" column in the October 1984 *Scientific American*.

or "i4mp2s4" if 1's are deleted) or by keeping a 26-integer vector telling how many times each letter occurs. Other applications of signatures include the Federal Bureau of Investigation's method for storing fingerprints and the Soundex heuristic for identifying names that sound alike but are spelled differently.

NAME	SOUNDEX SIGNATURE
Smith	s530
Smythe	s530
Schultz	s243
Shultz	s432

Knuth describes the Soundex method in Chapter 6 of his *Sorting and Searching*.

Problem Definition. The last column showed that determining what the user really wants to do is an essential part of programming. The theme of this column is the next step in problem definition: what primitives will we use to solve the problem? In each case the *aha!* insight defined a new basic operation to make the problem trivial.

A Problem Solver's Perspective. Good programmers are a little bit lazy: they sit back and wait for an insight rather than rushing forward with their first idea. That must, of course, be balanced with the initiative to code at the proper time. The real skill, though, is knowing the proper time. That judgment comes only with the experience of solving problems and reflecting on their solutions.

2.6 Problems

1. Consider the problem of finding all the anagrams of a given input word. How would you solve this problem given the word and the dictionary? What if you could spend some time and space to process the dictionary before answering any query?

2. Given a tape containing 1,050,000 twenty-bit integers, how can you find one that appears at least twice?

3. We studied two vector rotation algorithms that require subtle code; implement each as a program. How does the greatest common divisor of I and N appear in the analysis of each program?

4. Several readers pointed out that while all three rotation algorithms require time proportional to N, the juggling algorithm is apparently twice as fast as the reversal algorithm: it stores and retrieves each element of the array just once, while the reversal algorithm does so twice. I implemented both subroutines in the obvious ways and found that for small values of N, the routines took the same amount of CPU time; at $N=380,000$, both took 14 seconds. At $N=390,000$, though, the reversal routine took 16 seconds, while I aborted the juggling routine after an hour. Explain why the

observations of reality conflict with the simple theory. (Useful background: the machine had two megabytes of real memory, each array element required four bytes, and in the one hour run, I was 256.)

5. Vector rotation routines change the vector AB to BA; how would you transform the vector ABC to CBA? (This models the problem of swapping unequal-length blocks of memory.)

6. Bell Labs has a "user-operated directory assistance" program that allows employees to look up a number in a company telephone directory using a standard push-button telephone.

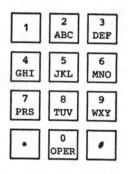

To find the number of the designer of the system, Mike Lesk, one dials the number of the service, types "LESK*M*" (that is, "5375*6*") and the system then speaks his number. One problem that arises in this system is that different names may have the same push-button encoding; when this happens in Lesk's system, it asks the user for more information. Given a large file of names, such as a standard metropolitan telephone directory, how would you locate these "false matches"? (When Lesk did this experiment on such a directory, he found that their incidence was just 0.2 percent.) How would you implement the routine that is given a push-button encoding of a name and returns either a name or an appropriate message?

7. In the early 1960's Vic Vyssotsky worked with a programmer who had to transpose a 4000-by-4000 matrix stored on magnetic tape (each record had the same several-dozen-byte format). The original program his colleague suggested would have taken fifty hours to run; how did Vyssotsky reduce the run time to half an hour?

8. [J. Ullman] Given a set of N real numbers, a real number T, and an integer K, how quickly can you determine whether there exists a K-element subset of the set that sums to at most T?

9. Sequential search and binary search represent a tradeoff between search time and preprocessing time. How many binary searches need be performed in an N-element table to buy back the preprocessing time required to sort the table?

10. On the first day a researcher worked with Thomas Edison, Edison asked him to compute the volume of an empty light bulb shell. After several hours with calipers and calculus, he returned with the answer of 150 cubic centimeters. In a few seconds, Edison computed and responded "closer to 155" — how did he do it? Give other examples of *aha!* insights in analog computation.

2.7 Further Reading

Knuth's seven-volume *Art of Computer Programming* is the definitive treatise on the field of algorithms. Three of the seven volumes have appeared so far: *Fundamental Algorithms* (published by Addison-Wesley in 1968, Second Edition 1973), *Seminumerical Algorithms* (1969, Second Edition 1981), and *Sorting and Searching* (1973, Second Printing 1975). These encyclopedic works contain virtually all that was known about their fields as of the publication dates. Most of the algorithms are presented in assembly code, thereby exposing many issues that arise in their implementation as programs.

Sedgewick's *Algorithms* (Addison-Wesley, 1983) is an excellent undergraduate text on the subject. It covers many algorithmic fields not yet described by Knuth and is more up to date on several others. Its intuitive approach is a boon for the practitioner interested in reducing algorithms to code.

2.8 Implementing an Anagram Program *[Sidebar]*†

I wrote my anagram program on the UNIX system, which is particularly supportive of the task. After you read about my program, think about how you would write a similar program on your favorite system. The program is organized as a three-stage "pipeline" in which the output of one program is fed as input to the next. The first program `sign`s the words, the second `sort`s the signed file, and the third `squash`es the words in an anagram class onto one line. Here's the process on a six-word dictionary.

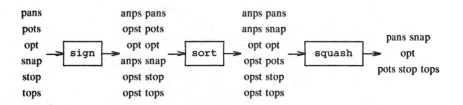

The output contains three anagram classes.

---

† Sidebars in *Communications of the ACM* are offset from the text of the column, often in a bar at the side of the page. While they aren't an essential part of the column, they provide perspective on the material. In this book they appear as the last section in a column, marked as a "sidebar".

The following `sign` program assumes that no word contains more than one hundred letters and that the input file contains only lower-case letters and new-line characters. (I therefore preprocessed the system dictionary with a one-line character transliteration program to change upper-case characters to lower case.)

```
#define WORDMAX 101
main( )
{    char thisword[WORDMAX], sig[WORDMAX];
     while (scanf("%s", thisword) != EOF) {
          strcpy(sig, thisword);
          qsort(sig, strlen(sig), 1, compchar);
          printf("%s %s\n", sig, thisword);
     }
}
```

The `while` loop reads a string into `thisword` until it comes to the end of the file. The `strcpy` routine copies the input word to the word `sig`, whose characters are then sorted by calling the system sort routine `qsort` (the parameters are the name of the array to be sorted, its length, the number of bytes per character, and the name of the routine to compare two characters). Finally, the `printf` statement prints the signature followed by the word itself and a newline character, \n.

The system `sort` program brings together all words with the same signature; the `squash` program prints them on a single line. It required just three lines in AWK, a pattern-action language designed for file manipulation.

```
$1 != prev    { prev = $1; if (NR > 1) printf "\n" }
              { printf "%s ", $2 }
   END        { printf "\n" }
```

The bulk of the work is performed by the second statement; for each input line, it writes out the second field ($2) followed by a space. The first line catches the changes: if the first field ($1) changes from `prev` (its previous value), then `prev` is reset and as long as this record isn't the first in the file (the number of the current record is NR), the newline character is printed. The third line is invoked at the end of the file; it writes a final newline character.

After testing those simple parts on small input files, I constructed the anagram list by typing

```
sign <dictionary | sort | squash >gramlist
```

That command feeds the file `dictionary` to the program `sign`, pipes `sign`'s output into `sort`, pipes `sort`'s output into `squash`, and writes `squash`'s output in the file `gramlist`. The whole effort took five executable lines of C code, three lines of AWK, and one command line; it is concise because the UNIX system provides a powerful set of languages and a convenient mechanism for linking together programs written in different languages. The program ran in 27 minutes: 6 in sign, 6 in sort and 15 in squash. I could have halved the total run time by recoding squash in C (interpreted AWK is typically an order of magnitude slower than C), but because this is a single-shot program it wasn't worth the effort.

I ran the program on the standard system dictionary, which contains 71,887 words; it does not, however, include many -s and -ed endings. The following were among the more interesting anagram classes.

```
subessential suitableness
canter centra nectar recant trance
caret cater crate react recta trace
destain instead sainted stained
adroitly dilatory idolatry
earthling haltering lathering
least setal slate stale steal stela teals
reins resin rinse risen serin siren
```

COLUMN 3: **DATA STRUCTURES PROGRAMS**

Most programmers have seen them, and most good programmers realize they've written at least one. They are huge, messy, ugly programs that should have been short, clean, beautiful programs. I once saw a COBOL program whose guts were

```
IF THISINPUT IS EQUAL TO 001 ADD 1 TO COUNT001.
IF THISINPUT IS EQUAL TO 002 ADD 1 TO COUNT002.
    ...
IF THISINPUT IS EQUAL TO 500 ADD 1 TO COUNT500.
```

Although the program actually accomplished a slightly more complicated task, it isn't misleading to view it as counting how many times each integer between 1 and 500 was found in a file. It contained about 1600 lines of code. 500 to define the variables COUNT001 through COUNT500, the above 500 to do the counting, 500 to print out how many times each integer was found, and 100 miscellaneous statements. Think for a minute about how you could accomplish the same task with a program just a tiny fraction of the size by using a different data structure — a 500-element array to replace the 500 individual variables. (Programmers who are paid per line of code may wish to ignore this exercise; managers who pay by the line may wish to faint.)

Hence the title of this column: a proper view of data does indeed structure programs. This column describes several medium-sized programs that were made smaller (and better) by restructuring their internal data. The programs were typically reduced from a few thousand to a few hundred lines. The principles also apply to large software systems: we'll see how proper data structure design helped to reduce the development time of one system from 250 staff-years to 80 staff-years.

3.1 A Survey Program

The next program we'll study summarized about twenty thousand questionnaires filled out by college students. A small part of the output looked like

	Total	US Citi	Perm Visa	Temp Visa	Male	Female
Afro Amer	1289	1239	17	2	684	593
Mex. Amer	675	577	80	11	448	219
Amer Ind.	198	182	5	3	132	64
Span Sur	411	223	152	20	224	179
Asian/PI	519	312	152	41	247	270
Caucasian	16272	15663	355	33	9367	6836
Other	225	123	78	19	129	92
Totals	19589	18319	839	129	11231	8253

For each ethnic group, the number of males plus the number of females is a little less than the total because some people didn't answer some questions. The real output was more complicated. I've shown all seven rows plus the total row, but only the six columns that represent the totals and two other categories, citizenship status and sex. In the real problem there were twenty-five columns that represented eight categories and three similar pages of output: one apiece for two separate campuses, and one for the sum of the two. There were also a few other closely related tables to be printed, such as the number of students that declined to answer each question. Each questionnaire was represented by a punched card in which the first column contained the ethnic group encoded as an integer between one and eight (for the seven categories and "refused"), the second column contained citizenship status, and so on through column nine.

The programmer coded the COBOL program from the systems analyst's flowchart; after working on it for two months and producing a thousand lines of code, he estimated that he was half done. I understood his predicament after I saw the five-page flowchart: the program was built around 350 distinct variables — 25 columns times 7 rows times 2 pages. After variable declarations, the program consisted of a rat's nest of logic that decided which variables to increment as each input record was read. Think for a minute about how you would write the program.

The crucial decision is that the numbers should be stored as an array. The next decision is harder: should the array be laid out according to its output structure (along the three dimensions of campus, ethnic group, and the twenty-five columns) or its input structure (along the four dimensions of campus, ethnic group, category, and value within category)? Ignoring the campus dimension, the approaches can be viewed as

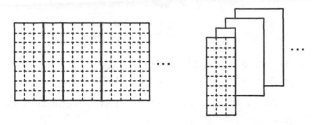

Both approaches work; the three-dimensional view in my program resulted in a little more work when the data was read and a little less work when it was written. The program took 150 lines of FORTRAN: 80 to build tables, 30 to produce the output I described, and 40 to produce other tables.

The count program and the survey program were two needlessly big programs; both contained numerous variables that were replaced by a single array. Reducing the length of the code by an order of magnitude led to correct programs that were developed quickly and could be easily tested and maintained. And although it didn't matter much in either application, both small programs were more efficient in run time and space than the big programs.

Why do programmers write big programs when small ones will do? One reason is that they lack the important laziness mentioned in Section 2.5; they rush ahead to code their first idea. But in both cases I've described, there was a deeper problem: the programmers thought about their problems in COBOL, and many COBOL programmers think of arrays as fixed tables that are initialized at the beginning of a program and never altered.

There are many other reasons that programmers make these mistakes. When I prepared to write this column I found a similar example in my own code for the survey program. The main input loop had forty lines of code in eight five-statement blocks, the first two of which could be expressed as

```
if InputColumn(2) = Refused then
    add 1 to Declined(EthnicGroup, 1)
  else
    ThisIndex := 1 + InputColumn(2)
    add 1 to Count(Campus, EthnicGroup, ThisIndex)
if InputColumn(3) = Refused then
    add 1 to Declined(EthnicGroup, 2)
  else
    ThisIndex := 4 + InputColumn(3)
    add 1 to Count(Campus, EthnicGroup, ThisIndex)
```

I could have replaced those forty lines with six, after initializing the array Offset to contain 1, 4, 6, ...

```
for I := 1 to 8 do
    if InputColumn(I+1) = Refused then
        add 1 to Declined(EthnicGroup, I)
    else
        ThisIndex := Offset(I) + InputColumn(I+1)
        add 1 to Count(Campus, EthnicGroup, ThisIndex)
```

I had been so satisfied to get one order-of-magnitude reduction in code length that I missed another one staring me in the face.

3.2 Form Letters

The next program is given a file of names and addresses and produces a customized form letter for each record in the file. For instance, given this input record with eight fields

```
Public|John Q.|Mr.|600|Maple Street|Your Town|Iowa|12345
```

(where "|" separates fields within a record), the program should produce the letter that starts

```
Mr. John Q. Public
600 Maple Street
Your Town, Iowa 12345

Dear Mr. Public:

I am sure that the Public family is anxious
to be the first family on Maple Street to own a
microprocessor-controlled clothesline.
```

This task is typical of many problems other than form letters: a little computation produces a lot of output.

The hasty programmer may be tempted to write a program that begins

```
loop until end of input
    read LastName, FirstName, Title, StreetNum,
         StreetName, Town, State, Zip
    skip to new page
    print Title, " ", FirstName, " ", LastName
    print StreetNum, " ", StreetName
    print Town, ", ", State, " ", Zip
    print
    print "Dear ", Title, " ", LastName
    print
    print "I am sure that the ", LastName, " family is anxious"
    print "to be the first family on ", StreetName, " to own a"
    print "microprocessor-controlled clothesline."
```

Such a program is tedious in a language that supports variable-length strings in input-output statements, and horrible in a language without that feature. In either case, maintaining the program is dreadful; adding a few words near the beginning of the paragraph could entail laboriously reformatting the entire paragraph by hand.

A more elegant approach involves writing a "form letter generator" that relies on a *form letter schema* like

```
$3 $2 $1
$4 $5
$6, $7 $8

Dear $3 $1:

I am sure that the $1 family is anxious
to be the first family on $5 to own a
microprocessor-controlled clothesline.
```

The notation $i refers to the ith field in the input record, so $1 is the last name, and so on. The schema is interpreted by the following pseudocode, which assumes that a literal $ character is written in the input schema as $$.

```
read Schema from schema file
loop until end of input file
    for I := 1 to NumFields do
        read Field[I] from input file
    skip to new page
    loop from start to end of Schema
        C := next character in Schema
        if C ≠ "$" then
            printchar C
        else
            C := next character in Schema
            case C of
                "$":        printchar "$"
                "1" - "9":  printstring Field[C]
                other:      Error("Bad Schema")
```

The schema is represented in the program as one long array of characters in which text lines are ended by "new line" characters. As before, the interpreter is easy to implement if the language supports variable-length strings and harder if it doesn't. Even so, variable-length strings must now be handled in only one place rather than at each occurrence in the schema.

With a language that supports variable-length output strings, writing the generator and the schema may be a little more work than writing the obvious program. Under many circumstances, though, that extra work will pay off handsomely: if the letter is redesigned then the schema can be manipulated with a text editor, and the second form letter will be simple indeed to prepare.

The concept of a report schema could have greatly simplified a 5300-line COBOL program I once maintained. The program's input was a description of a family's financial status; its output was a booklet summarizing the status and recommending future policy. Some numbers: 120 input fields on 10 cards; 400 output lines on 18 pages; 300 lines of code to clean the input data, 800 lines for computation, and 4200 lines to write the output. In one place the program used 113 lines of code to write in the middle of a line a string whose length varied between one and ten characters. I estimate that the 4200 lines of output code could have been replaced by an interpreter of at most a couple hundred lines of COBOL (and far fewer in a modern language) and a schema of 400 lines. Originally writing the program in that form would have resulted in code that was at most one-third the size and much easier to maintain.

3.3 An Array of Examples

Line Printer Graphics. A series of print statements is almost always the wrong way to solve the time-honored problem of drawing amusing pictures in a 66×132 (or 24×80, or ...) matrix of characters. Some kinds of structure can be captured in a short mathematical expression; this sine wave can be described in just a few lines of code on many systems.

Less regular pictures can be described by an array of key locations. Arbitrary pictures are often best represented by an array; this is a 48×48 array of blanks and the character "x".

Problem 3 stores pictures by mixing and matching these representations.

Error Messages. Dirty systems have hundreds of error messages scattered throughout the code, mixed in with other print statements; clean systems have them accessed through a single routine. Consider the difficulty of answering the following requests under the "dirty" and "clean" organizations: produce a list of all possible error messages, change each error that requires operator intervention to ring the console bell, and translate the error messages into French or German.

Date Routines. Given a year and day of the year, return the month and day of the month; for instance, the 61st day of 1988 is the 1st day of the 3rd month. In their *Elements of Programming Style* (Second Edition, pp. 52-54)†, Kernighan and Plauger present a fifty-five line program for this task taken straight from someone else's programming text. They then give a five-line program for the task, using an array of twenty-six integers. Several representation issues arise in date routines, such as determining whether a given year is a leap year and representing the number of days per month; see Problem 4.

Word Analysis. There are many computing problems in the analysis of English words. In Column 13, for instance, we'll study a spelling checker that uses "suffix stripping" to condense its dictionary: it stores the single word "laugh" without storing all its various endings ("-ing", "-s", "-ed", etc.). Linguists have developed a substantial body of rules for such tasks. Doug McIlroy knew that code was the wrong vessel for such rules when he wrote a program that speaks individual words on a voice synthesizer; he instead wrote it using twenty pages of code and an eight-page table. When someone modified the program without adding to the tables, that resulted in fifty extra pages of code to do twenty percent more work. McIlroy asserts that he could probably do the expanded task now using fewer than twenty pages by adding even more tables. To try your own hand on a similar set of rules, see Problem 5.

Terminal Problems. Proper data structure design can help reduce the mountains of code typically used to deal with terminals. Many terminals support such operations as writing over existing screen characters and moving lines around the screen without retransmitting characters; these features greatly increase the speed and ease of use of modern text editors. Several approaches to using such features are only marginally better than ignoring them: one approach is to write a different program for each terminal type, another is to have a huge case statement at each place the program does input or output. The UNIX system solves the problem with a "terminal capability" database that gives a programmer uniform access to the capabilities. This database presents the abstract specification of a feature (such as moving lines on the screen) and hides its implementation in a particular terminal (the character sequence that moves the lines); programs written for the one "virtual terminal" run on any terminal in the database.

---

† Pages 48 through 58 of *The Elements of Programming Style* contain a lovely collection of small programs in which restructuring data leads to clean code. The philosophy in Kernighan and Plauger's *Software Tools* removes much of the temptation to write messy code: the programmer's job is to build a clean and powerful tool, which users then apply to their problems.

3.4 A Big Program

We've seen a variety of simple data structures that provide elegant solutions to hard problems. There's a message in that pattern: the contribution of computer science to software is often through simple ideas. But every now and then a theoretical breakthrough shakes the practitioner's world, and this column wouldn't be complete without one such story about data structures. I'll tell an abbreviated version of a story told in full by A. Jay Goldstein in his excellent article "A directed hypergraph database: a model for the local loop telephone plant" in *The Bell System Technical Journal 61*, 9, November 1982 (pp. 2529-2554).

Telephone operating companies refer to part of their equipment outside the central office as the "local loop plant" — that term includes cables, distribution terminals, cross-connect terminals, wires, etc. Information about the local loop plant is stored in a database for purposes of "building" loops to satisfy customer service requests and performing various maintenance operations.

A Bell Labs development group of about two hundred professionals spent five years implementing such a database for telephone operating companies. About fifty people were involved with the local loop plant part of the project throughout the five years; that part of the final system consisted of 155,000 lines of COBOL. The system was used in the field by an operating company, but it had many faults: it was slow, extremely difficult to maintain, and almost impossible to extend as new telephone technology was deployed. In retrospect, many of the faults could be traced to the data structure on which the system was built: a CODASYL database consisting of four hundred record schemas, printed in a four-inch-thick line printer listing.

For a number of reasons, the complete system was redone as three systems, one of which dealt with the local loop plant. That system is the topic of Goldstein's paper. The first stage in its design was the development of a sound mathematical model of the local loop plant. The development team then built a special-purpose database management system that reflects the model. The model and system are a special form of an entity-relationship database: a directed hypergraph in which vertices are objects in the local loop plant (connectors, cables, living units, etc.) and the directed edges denote logical relationships between objects. This structure allows a great deal of flexibility in incorporating into the system new devices and new interconnections of devices; it also helps solve the nasty problems of dealing with "pending" operations that have been scheduled but not yet executed. The new database was described with just forty schemas in less than half an inch of line printer listing. With this data structure at its heart, the complete system was developed and delivered in three years, with a staff of about thirty.

The new system is clearly superior to its predecessor. It was developed in about half the calendar time and with about half the staff devoted to the old system. The new system is a delight to maintain: there are an order of magnitude fewer bug reports coming in from the field, and changes that previously required months can now be accomplished in days. The maintenance staff of the old system had fifty people; the new system is maintained by five. The new system is more efficient in run time and more easily extensible to incorporate new telephone technologies. The differences show in the field: while the old system had several failures per week that required rebooting, the new system did not experience one such failure in the two years following initial testing. The new system is used by several operating companies.

Many factors contributed to the success of the new system. As a second system, it started with a clear problem definition and knowledge of what was successful in a previous implementation. It was written in a modern programming language and was developed using information-hiding programming methodologies. But of the many strong attributes of the new system, the one that I have heard mentioned most often is the clean conceptual model and database on which it is built. While the previous designers started by thinking in CODASYL terms and tried to force their problem into that world, the second group started with a solid view of the data and used that to structure the program. An additional benefit of the approach is that the designers, implementers and users can talk to one another in the single common language implied by the world view.

3.5 Principles

The moral of each of the stories is the same: *don't write a big program when a little one will do*. Most of the structures exemplify what Polya calls the Inventor's Paradox in his *How To Solve It*: "the more general problem may be easier to solve". In programming this means that it may be harder to solve a 73-case problem directly than to write a general program to handle the N-case version, and then apply it to the case that $N = 73$.

This column has concentrated on just one contribution that data structures can make to software: reducing big programs to small programs. Data structure design can have many other positive impacts, including time and space reduction and increased portability and maintainability. Fred Brooks's comment in Chapter 9 of his *Mythical Man Month* is stated for space reduction, but it is good advice for programmers who desire the other attributes as well:

> The programmer at wit's end for lack of space can often do best by disentangling himself from his code, rearing back, and contemplating his data. Representation *is* the essence of programming.

Here are a few principles for you to ponder as you rear back.

Rework repeated code into arrays. A long stretch of similar code is often best expressed by the simplest of data structures, the array.

Be familiar with advanced data structures. Advanced data structures aren't appropriate very often, but when you need them, they're indispensable.

Let the data structure the program. The theme of this column is that data can structure a program by replacing complicated code by a data structure. There are many other interpretations of the advice. David Parnas has demonstrated that the data a program contains gives deep insight into a good module structure for the program (see "On the criteria to be used in decomposing systems into modules" in the December 1972 *Communications of the ACM*); we will return to this topic as we study "abstract data types" in Columns 11 and 12. Michael Jackson argues persuasively that for many common tasks in business data processing, a thorough understanding of the input and output data can almost automatically lead to code (see *Principles of Program Design*, published in 1975 by Academic Press). Although the particulars change, the theme remains: before writing code, good programmers thoroughly understand the input, the output, and the intermediate data structures around which their programs are built.

3.6 Problems

1. A programming text gives the following twenty-five **if** statements as a reasonable approach for calculating the 1978 United States Federal Income Tax. The rate sequence .14, .15, .16, .17, ... exhibits jumps larger than .01 later in the sequence. Any comments?

```
·if Income <= 2200 then
    Tax := 0
  else if Income <= 2700 then
    Tax :=          .14 * (Income - 2200)
  else if Income <= 3200 then
    Tax :=     70 + .15 * (Income - 2700)
  else if Income <= 3700 then
    Tax :=    145 + .16 * (Income - 3200)
  else if Income <= 4200 then
    Tax :=    225 + .17 * (Income - 3700)
    ...
  else
    Tax := 53090 + .70 * (Income - 102200)
```

2. A kth-order linear recurrence with constant coefficients defines a series as

$$a_n = c_1 a_{n-1} + c_2 a_{n-2} + \cdots + c_k a_{n-k} + c_{k+1},$$

where $c_1, \ldots, c_{k+1}$ are real numbers. Write a program that with input k, $a_1, \ldots, a_k, c_1, \ldots, c_{k+1}$, and N produces the output a_1 through a_N. How difficult is that program compared to a program that solves one particular fifth-order recurrence, but does so without using arrays?

3. Write a "banner" procedure that is given a capital letter as input and produces as output an array of characters that graphically depicts that letter.

4. Write procedures for the following date problems: given two dates, compute

the number of days between them; given a date, return its day of the week; given a month and year, produce a calendar for the month as an array of characters. The first version of your programs may assume that the year is in the 1900's; the second version should be as general as possible.

5. This problem deals with a small part of the problem of hyphenating English words. The following list of rules describes some legal hyphenations of words that end in the letter "c":

   > et-ic al-is-tic s-tic p-tic -lyt-ic ot-ic an-tic n-tic c-tic at-ic h-nic n-ic m-ic l-lic b-lic -clic l-ic h-ic f-ic d-ic -bic a-ic -mac i-ac

   The rules must be applied in the above order; thus the hyphenations "eth-nic" (which is caught by the rule "h-nic") and "clinic" (which fails that test and falls through to "n-ic"). How would you represent such rules in a subroutine that is given a word and must return suffix hyphenations?

6. Write a form letter generator that is general enough to interpret the schema we saw earlier; make your program as simple as possible. Design small schemas and input files to test the correctness of your program.

7. Typical dictionaries allow one to look up the definition of a word, and Problem 2.1 describes a dictionary that allows one to look up the anagrams of a word. Design dictionaries for looking up the proper spelling of a word and for looking up the rhymes of a word. Discuss dictionaries for looking up an integer sequence (such as 1, 1, 2, 3, 5, 8, ...), a chemical structure, or the metrical structure of a song.

8. The arrays in this column have integer indices. Some languages, such as SNOBOL and AWK, have "associative arrays" with string indices, and therefore allow assignments like *count*["*cat*"]:=7. How could you use such arrays? How would you implement them?

9. [S. C. Johnson] Seven-segment devices provide an inexpensive display of decimal digits:

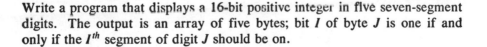

The seven segments are usually numbered as

$$\begin{array}{c} 2 \\ 3\ |\ _1\ |\ 4 \\ 5\ |\ _0\ |\ 6 \end{array}$$

Write a program that displays a 16-bit positive integer in five seven-segment digits. The output is an array of five bytes; bit I of byte J is one if and only if the Ith segment of digit J should be on.

3.7 Further Reading

The structure of data is intimately related to the algorithms that operate on it; the algorithms texts cited in Section 2.7 contain a wealth of information about data structures. Beyond those books, Standish's *Data Structure Techniques* (published in 1980 by Addison-Wesley) is a thorough and readable reference.

COLUMN 4: **WRITING CORRECT PROGRAMS**

In the late 1960's people were talking about the promise of programs that verify the correctness of other programs. Unfortunately, in the late 1980's, with precious few exceptions, there is still little more than talk about automated verification systems. Despite unrealized expectations, however, research on program verification has given us something more valuable than a black box that gobbles programs and flashes "good" or "bad" — we now have a fundamental understanding of computer programming.

The purpose of this column is to show how that fundamental understanding can help programmers write correct programs. But before we get to the subject itself, we must keep it in perspective. Coding skill is just one small part of writing correct programs. The majority of the task is the subject of the three previous columns. problem definition, algorithm design, and data structure selection. If you perform those tasks well, writing correct code is usually easy.

4.1 The Challenge of Binary Search

Even with the best of designs, every now and then a programmer has to write subtle code. This column is about one problem that requires particularly careful code: binary search. After reviewing the problem and sketching an algorithm, we'll use verification principles as we write the program.

We first met this problem in Section 2.2; we are to determine whether the sorted array $X[1..N]$ contains the element T. Precisely, we know that $N \geq 0$ and that $X[1] \leq X[2] \leq ... \leq X[N]$; when $N=0$ the array is empty. The types of T and the elements of X are the same; the pseudocode should work equally well for integers, reals or strings. The answer is stored in the integer P (for position): when P is zero T is not in $X[1..N]$, otherwise $1 \leq P \leq N$ and $T=X[P]$.

Binary search solves the problem by keeping track of a range within the array in which T must be if it is anywhere in the array.† Initially, the range is

---

† Bill McKeeman of the Wang Institute of Graduate Studies noted that this description avoids several common problems in coding binary search. His formal derivation of a similar high-level description appears in "Programming Pearls" on pages 631-632 of the July 1984 *Communications of the ACM*.

the entire array. The range is shrunk by comparing its middle element to *T* and discarding half the range. The process continues until *T* is discovered in the array or until the range in which it must lie is known to be empty. In an *N*-element table, the search uses roughly $\log_2 N$ comparisons.

Most programmers think that with the above description in hand, writing the code is easy; they're wrong. The only way you'll believe this is by putting down this column right now, and writing the code yourself. Try it.

I've assigned this problem in courses at Bell Labs and IBM. Professional programmers had a couple of hours to convert the above description into a program in the language of their choice; a high-level pseudocode was fine. At the end of the specified time, almost all the programmers reported that they had correct code for the task. We would then take thirty minutes to examine their code, which the programmers did with test cases. In several classes and with over a hundred programmers, the results varied little: ninety percent of the programmers found bugs in their programs (and I wasn't always convinced of the correctness of the code in which no bugs were found).

I was amazed: given ample time, only about ten percent of professional programmers were able to get this small program right. But they aren't the only ones to find this task difficult: in the history in Section 6.2.1 of his *Sorting and Searching*, Knuth points out that while the first binary search was published in 1946, the first published binary search without bugs did not appear until 1962.

4.2 Writing the Program

The key idea of binary search is that we always know that if *T* is anywhere in $X[1..N]$, then it must be in a certain range of *X*. We'll use the shorthand *MustBe(range)* to mean that if *T* is anywhere in the array, then it must be in *range*. We can use this notation to convert the above description of binary search into a program sketch.

```
initialize range to 1..N
loop
    { Invariant: MustBe(range) }
    if range is empty,
        return that T is nowhere in the array
    compute M, the middle of the range
    use M as a probe to shrink the range
        if T is found during the shrinking process,
        return its position
```

The crucial part of this program is the *loop invariant*, which is enclosed in { }'s. This *assertion* about the program state is called an *invariant* because it is true at the beginning and end of each iteration of the loop; it formalizes the intuitive notion we had above.

We'll now refine the program, making sure that all actions respect the invariant. The first issue we must face is the representation of *range*: we'll use two indices *L* and *U* (for "lower" and "upper") to represent the range *L..U*. (There are other possible representations for a range, such as its beginning position and its length.) The next step is the initialization; what values should *L* and *U* have so that *MustBe(L,U)* is true? The obvious choice is 1 and *N*: *MustBe(1,N)* says that if *T* is anywhere in *X*, then it is in *X*[1..*N*], which is precisely what we know at the beginning of the program. Initialization therefore consists of the assignments L:=1 and U:=N.

The next tasks are to check for an empty range and to compute the new midpoint, *M*. The range *L..U* is empty if *L>U*, in which case we store the special value 0 in *P* and terminate the loop, which gives

```
if L > U then
    P := 0; break
```

The break statement terminates the enclosing loop. This statement computes *M*, the midpoint of the range·

```
M := (L+U) div 2
```

The *div* operator implements integer division: 6 *div* 2 is 3, as is 7 *div* 2. The program is now

```
L := 1; U := N
loop
    { Invariant: MustBe(L,U) }
    if L > U then
        P := 0; break
    M := (L+U) div 2
    use M as a probe to shrink the range L..U
        if T is found during the shrinking process,
        note its position and break
```

Refining the last three lines in the loop body will involve comparing *T* and *X*[*M*] and taking appropriate action to maintain the invariant. Thus the code will have the form

```
case
    X[M] < T:   Action A
    X[M] = T:   Action B
    X[M] > T:   Action C
```

For Action B, we know that T is in position M, so we set P to M and **break** the loop. Because the other two cases are symmetric, we'll focus on the first and trust that the last will follow by symmetry (this is part of the reason we'll verify the code precisely in the next section).

If $X[M]<T$, then we know that $X[1]\leq X[2]\leq ...\leq X[M]<T$, so T can't be anywhere in $X[1..M]$. Combining this with the knowledge that T is not outside $X[L..U]$, we know that if it is anywhere, then it must be in $X[M+1..U]$, which we write as $MustBe(M+1,U)$. We then reestablish the invariant $MustBe(L,U)$ by setting L to $M+1$. Putting these cases into the previous code sketch gives the final routine.

```
L := 1; U := N
loop
    { MustBe(L,U) }
    if L > U then
        P := 0; break
    M := (L+U) div 2
    case
        X[M] < T:   L := M+1
        X[M] = T:   P := M; break
        X[M] > T:   U := M-1
```

It's a short program: ten lines of code and one invariant assertion. The basic techniques of program verification — stating the invariant precisely and keeping an eye towards maintaining the invariant as we wrote each line of code — helped us greatly as we converted the algorithm sketch into pseudocode. This process gives us some confidence in the program, but we are by no means certain of its correctness. Spend a few minutes convincing yourself that the code behaves as specified before reading further.

4.3 Understanding the Program

When I face a subtle programming problem, I try to derive code at about the level of detail we just saw. I then use verification methods to increase my confidence that it is correct. We'll use verification at this level in Columns 8, 10 and 12.

In this section we'll study a verification argument for the binary search code at a picky level of detail — in practice I'd do a much less formal analysis. The version of the program on the next page is (far too) heavily annotated with assertions that formalize the intuitive notions that we used as we originally wrote the code.

While the development of the code was top-down (starting with the general idea and refining it to individual lines of code), this analysis of correctness will be bottom-up: we'll see how the individual lines of code work together to solve the problem.

Warning
Boring material ahead.
Skip to Section 4.4
when drowsiness strikes.

We'll start with lines 1 through 3. The assertion in line 1 that $MustBe(1,N)$ is true by the definition of $MustBe$: if T is anywhere in the array, then it must be in $X[1..N]$. The assignments in line 2 of $L:=1$ and $U:=N$ therefore give the assertion in line 3: $MustBe(L,U)$.

We come now to the hard part: the loop in lines 4 through 27. There are three parts to our argument for its correctness, each of which is closely related to the loop invariant:

Initialization. The invariant is true when the loop is executed for the first time.

Preservation. If the invariant holds at the beginning of an iteration and the loop body is executed, then the invariant will remain true after the loop body finishes execution.

Termination. The loop will terminate and the desired result will hold (in this case, the desired result is that P have the correct value). Showing this will use the facts established by the invariant.

For initialization we note that the assertion in line 3 is the same as that in line 5. To establish the other two properties, we'll reason from line 5 through to line 27. When we discuss lines 9 and 21 (the break statements) we will establish termination properties, and if we make it all the way to line 27, we will have established preservation, because it is the same as line 5.

```
 1.    { MustBe(1,N) }
 2.    L := 1; U := N
 3.    { MustBe(L,U) }
 4.    loop
 5.        { MustBe(L,U) }
 6.        if L > U then
 7.            { L > U and MustBe(L,U) }
 8.            { T is nowhere in the array }
 9.            P := 0; break
10.        { MustBe(L,U) and L <= U }
11.        M := (L+U) div 2
12.        { MustBe(L,U) and L <= M <= U }
13.        case
14.            X[M] < T:
15.                    { MustBe(L,U) and CantBe(1,M) }
16.                    { MustBe(M+1,U) }
17.                    L := M+1
18.                    { MustBe(L,U) }
19.            X[M] = T:
20.                    { X[M] = T }
21.                    P := M; break
22.            X[M] > T:
23.                    { MustBe(L,U) and CantBe(M,N) }
24.                    { MustBe(L,M-1) }
25.                    U := M-1
26.                    { MustBe(L,U) }
27.        { MustBe(L,U) }
```

A successful test in line 6 yields the assertion of line 7: if T is anywhere in the array then it must be between L and U, and $L>U$. Those facts imply line 8: T is nowhere in the array. We thus correctly terminate the loop in line 9 after setting P to zero.

If the test in line 6 fails, we come to line 10. The invariant still holds (we've done nothing to change it), and because the test failed we know that $L \leq U$. Line 11 sets M to the average of L and U, truncated down to the nearest integer. Because the average is always between the two values and truncating can't move it below L, we have the assertion of line 12.

The analysis of the case statement in lines 13 through 27 considers each of its three possible choices. The easiest choice to analyze is the second alternative, in line 19. Because of the assertion in line 20, we are correct in setting P to M and terminating the loop. This is the second of two places where the loop is terminated, and both end it correctly, so we have established the termination correctness of the loop.

We come next to the two symmetric branches of the case statement; because we concentrated on the first branch as we developed the code, we'll turn our attention now to lines 22 through 26. Consider the assertion in line 23. The first clause is the invariant, which the program has not altered. The second clause is true because $T<X[M]\leq X[M+1]\leq...\leq X[N]$, so we know that T can't be anywhere in the array above position $M-1$; this is expressed with the shorthand $CantBe(M,N)$. Logic tells us that if T must be between L and U and can't be at or above M, then it must be between L and $M-1$ (if it is anywhere in X); hence line 24. Execution of line 25 with line 24 true leaves line 26 true — that is the definition of assignment. This choice of the case statement therefore re-establishes the invariant in line 27.

The argument for lines 14 through 18 has exactly the same form, so we've analyzed all three choices of the case statement. One correctly terminates the loop, and the other two maintain the invariant.

This analysis of the code shows that if the loop terminates, then it does so with the correct value in P. It may still, however, have an infinite loop; indeed, that was the most common error in the programs written by the professional programmers.

Our halting proof uses a different aspect of the range $L..U$. That range is initially a certain finite size (N), and lines 6 through 9 ensure that the loop terminates when the range contains less than one element. To prove termination we therefore have to show that the range shrinks during each iteration of the loop. Line 12 tells us that M is always within the current range. Both looping branches of the case statement (lines 14 and 22) exclude the value at position M from the current range and thereby decrease its size by at least one. The program must therefore halt.

4.4 Implementing the Program

So far we've worked with the program in a high-level pseudo-language; our willingness to use suitable control structures allowed us to ignore the details of any particular implementation language and to focus on the heart of the problem. Eventually, though, we have to write the program in a real language. Just so you don't think that I chose the language to make the task easy, I implemented binary search in BASIC. Although that language is fine for some tasks, its paucity of control structures and its global (and typically short) variable names are substantial barriers to building real programs.

Even with these problems, the above pseudocode can be easily expressed in a BASIC dialect. Lines 1010 through 1045 provide a concise specification of the routine.

```
1000 '
1010 ' BINARY SEARCH FOR T IN X(1..N)
1020 '   PRE:  X(1..N) IS SORTED IN NONDECREASING ORDER
1030 '   POST: P=0  => T IS NOT IN X(1..N)
1040 '         P>0  => P<N+1 AND X(P)=T
1045 '   SIDE EFFECTS: L, U AND M ARE ALTERED
1050 '
1060 L=1: U=N
1070 ' MAIN LOOP
1080     ' INVARIANT: IF T IS ANYWHERE IN THE ARRAY,
1090     '               THEN IT MUST BE IN X(L..U)
1100     IF L>U THEN P=0: RETURN
1110     M=CINT((L+U)/2)
1120     IF X(M)<T THEN L=M+1: GOTO 1070
1130     IF X(M)>T THEN U=M-1: GOTO 1070
1140     '  X(M)=T
1150              P=M:    RETURN
```

Because I translated this program from the carefully verified pseudocode, I had good reason to believe that it is correct. Before I would use it in an application (or publish it), though, I would test it. I therefore wrote a simple test program in about twenty-five lines of BASIC, with the following structure.

```
declare X[0..11]
for I := 0 to 11 do X[I] := I
for N := 0 to 10 do
    print N
    for I := 1 to N do
        Assert(BSearch(I)    = I)
        Assert(BSearch(I-.5) = 0)
        Assert(BSearch(I+.5) = 0)
    Assert(BSearch(0)   = 0)
    Assert(BSearch(N+1) = 0)
```

The Assert routine does nothing if its argument is true but complains loudly if it is false. The first version of the program passed this test without incident.

These tests poke around most of the program. They test every possible position for successful and unsuccessful searches, and the case that an element is in the array but outside the search bounds. Testing N from zero to ten covers the empty array, common sizes for bugs (one, two and three), several powers of two, and many numbers one away from a power of two. The tests would have been dreadfully boring (and therefore probably erroneous) by hand, but they used an insignificant amount of computer time.

Many factors contribute to my opinion that the BASIC program is correct: I used sound principles to derive the pseudocode, I used analytic techniques to "verify" its correctness, and then I let a computer do what it's good at and bombard the program with test cases.

4.5 Principles

This exercise displays many strengths of program verification: the problem is important and requires careful code, the development of the program is guided by verification ideas, and the analysis of correctness employs general tools. The primary weakness of this exercise is its level of detail; in practice I would work at a less formal level. Fortunately, the details illustrate a number of general principles, including the following.

Assertions. The relations among input, program variables, and output describe the "state" of a program; assertions allow a programmer to enunciate those relations precisely. Their roles throughout a program's life are discussed in the next section.

Sequential Control Structures. The simplest structure to control a program is of the form "do this statement then that statement". We understand such structures by placing assertions between them and analyzing each step of the program's progress individually.

Selection Control Structures. These structures include `if` and `case` statements of various forms; during execution, one of many choices is selected. We show the correctness of such a structure by considering each of the several choices individually. The fact that a certain choice is selected allows us to make an assertion in the proof; if we execute the statement following `if I>J`, for instance, we can assert that $I>J$ and use that fact to derive the next relevant assertion.

Iteration Control Structures. There are three stages in arguing the correctness of a loop:

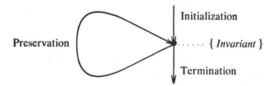

We first argue that the loop invariant is established by initialization, and then show that each iteration preserves its truth. These two steps show by mathematical induction that the invariant is true before and after each iteration of the loop. The third step is to argue that whenever execution of the loop terminates, the desired result is true. Together these establish that if the loop ever halts, then it does so correctly; we must prove that it does terminate by other means (the halting proof of binary search used a typical argument).

Subroutines. To verify a subroutine, we first state its purpose by two assertions. Its *precondition* is the state that must be true before it is called, and its *postcondition* is what the routine will guarantee on termination; the BASIC binary search in Section 4.4 provides examples. These conditions are more a contract than a statement of fact: they say that if the routine is called with the preconditions satisfied, then execution of the routine will establish its postcondition. After I prove once that the body of the routine has this property, I can use the stated relations between the pre- and postconditions without ever again considering the implementation.

4.6 The Roles of Program Verification

When one programmer tries to convince another that a piece of code is correct, the primary tool is the test case: execute the program by hand on a certain input. That's a powerful tool: it's good for detecting bugs, easy to use, and well understood. It is clear, however, that programmers have a deeper understanding of programs — if they didn't, they could never write them in the first place. One of the major benefits of program verification is that it gives programmers a language in which they can express that understanding.

Later in this book, especially in Columns 8, 10 and 12, we'll use verification techniques as we develop subtle programs. We'll use the language of verification to explain every line of code as it is written; it is particularly helpful to sketch an invariant for each loop. The important explanations end up in the program text as assertions; deciding which assertions to include is an art that comes only with practice.

The `Assert` statement illustrated in the test of binary search allows the assertions to be checked during testing, as in Solution 12.10. If a false assertion is encountered, then it is reported and the run is terminated (most systems allow assertion checking to be turned off if it is too costly in run time). All programs that appear later in this book have undergone tests like the one in Section 4.4. Details on those tests are in "Programming Pearls" in the July 1985 *Communications of the ACM*.

The language of verification is used often after the code is first written, starting during code walk-throughs. During testing, violations of the `Assert` statements point the way to bugs, and examining the form of a violation shows how to remove one bug without introducing another. When you debug, fix both the code and the false assertion: understand the code at all times, and resist those foul urges to "just change it until it works". Assertions are crucial during maintenance of a program; when you pick up code that you've never seen before, and no one else has looked at for years, assertions about the program state can give invaluable insight.

I mentioned before that these techniques are only a small part of writing correct programs; keeping the code simple is usually the key to correctness. On the other hand, several professional programmers familiar with these techniques have related to me an experience that is too common in my own programming: when they construct a program, the "hard" parts work the first time, while the bugs are in the "easy" parts. When they came to a hard part, they hunkered down and successfully used powerful formal techniques. In the easy parts, though, they returned to their old ways of programming, with the old results. I wouldn't have believed this phenomenon until it happened to me; such embarrassments are good motivation to use the techniques frequently.

4.7 Problems

1. As laborious as our proof of binary search was, it is still unfinished by some standards. How would you prove that the program is free of run-time errors (such as division by zero, word overflow, variables out of declared range, or array indices out of bounds)? If you have a background in discrete mathematics, can you formalize the proof in a logical system?

2. If the original binary search was too easy for you, try the variant that returns in P the first occurrence of T in the array X (if there are multiple occurrences of T, the original algorithm returns an arbitrary one). Your code should make a logarithmic number of comparisons of array elements; it is possible to do the job in $\log_2 N$ such comparisons.

3. Write and verify a recursive binary search program. Which parts of the code and proof stay the same as in the iterative version, and which parts change?

4. Add fictitious "timing variables" to your binary search program to count the number of comparisons it makes, and use program verification techniques to prove that its run time is indeed logarithmic.

5. Prove that this program terminates when its input is a positive integer.

```
read X
while X ≠ 1 do
    if Even(X) then X := X/2 else X := 3*X+1
```

6. [C. Scholten] David Gries calls this the "Coffee Can Problem" in his *Science of Programming*. You are initially given a coffee can that contains some black beans and some white beans and a large pile of "extra" black beans. You then repeat the following process until there is a single bean left in the can.

    Randomly select two beans from the can. If they are the same color, throw them both out and insert an extra black bean. If they are different colors, return the white bean to the can and throw out the black.

    Prove that the process terminates. What can you say about the color of the final remaining bean as a function of the numbers of black and white beans originally in the can?

7. A colleague faced the following problem in a program to draw lines on a bitmapped display. An array of N pairs of reals (a_i, b_i) defined the N lines $y_i = a_i x + b_i$. The lines were ordered in the x-interval $[0,1]$ in the sense that $y_i < y_{i+1}$ for all values of i between 1 and $N-1$ and all values of x in $[0,1]$:

Less formally, the lines don't touch in the vertical slabs. Given a point (x,y), where $0 \le x \le 1$, he wanted to determine the two lines that bracket the point. How could he solve the problem quickly?

8. Binary search is fundamentally faster than sequential search: to search an N-element table, it makes roughly $\log_2 N$ comparisons while sequential search makes roughly $N/2$. While it is often fast enough, in a few cases binary search must be made faster yet. Although you can't reduce the logarithmic number of comparisons made by the algorithm, can you rewrite the binary search code to be faster? For definiteness, assume that you are to search a sorted table of $N = 1000$ integers.

9. As exercises in program verification, precisely specify the input/output behavior of each of the following program fragments and show that the code meets its specification. The first program implements the vector addition $A := B + C$.

```
I := 1
while I <= N do
    A[I] := B[I] + C[I]
    I := I+1
```

The next fragment computes the maximum value in the vector X.

```
I := 2
Max := X[1]
while I <= N do
    if X[I] > Max then Max := X[I]
    I := I+1
```

This sequential search program returns the position of the first occurrence of T in the vector $X[1..N]$. The and in the while statement is conditional, like all ands and ors later in this book: if the first clause is false, then the second isn't evaluated.

```
I := 1
while I <= N and X[I] ≠ T do
    I := I+1
if I > N then P := 0 else P := I
```

This program computes the Nth power of X in time proportional to the logarithm of N. This recursive program is straightforward to code and to verify; the iterative version is subtle, and is left as an additional problem.

```
function Exp(X,N)
        pre  N >= 0
        post result = X**N
   if N = 0 then
      return 1
   else if Even(N) then  ·
      return Square(Exp(X,N/2))
   else
      return X*Exp(X,N-1)
```

10. Introduce errors into the binary search routine and see how they are caught by verification and by testing.

4.8 Further Reading

The notion of developing a program hand-in-hand with its proof of correctness was championed by E. W. Dijkstra in the early 1970's. *The Science of Programming* by David Gries (published by Springer-Verlag in 1981) is an excellent introduction to the field. It starts with a tutorial on logic, goes on to a formal view of program verification and development, and finally discusses programming in common languages. In this column I've tried to sketch the potential benefits of verification; the only way that most programmers will be able to use verification effectively is to study a book like Gries's.

4.9 Industrial-Strength Program Verification *[Sidebar]*

The verification techniques in this column can have an immediate impact on any programmer: carefully specify the input and output conditions of every module you write, and then use informal tools to develop the code and "verify" its correctness. Remember that verification is only one of many activities to ensure that you deliver correct, robust code; testing and debugging play an important role in any real system. A book like Gries's is bound to increase the quality of your code.

Harlan Mills describes the impact that verification techniques have had on IBM's Federal Systems Division in a special issue of the *IBM Systems Journal* devoted to software development (Volume 19, Number 4, 1980). Verification is a substantial part of a course required of all programmers in the division; the course is based on the book *Structured Programming* by Linger, Mills and Witt (published in 1979 by Addison-Wesley). Mills describes how techniques based on verification have played an important role in the division's timely delivery of substantial software: one project he describes delivered three million words of code and data (developed with 200 staff-years) on time and under budget. For more details on this effort and others within IBM, see that issue of the *Systems Journal*.

Although they are not yet ready to be used in most production environments, program verification systems may someday routinely assist the development of certain kinds of software. Excellent work in this area has been done at a number of centers; the Gypsy system developed at the University of Texas at Austin by a team led by Don Good is typical of this research.

Gypsy is a methodology for specifying, implementing, and proving the correctness of programs. At its heart is the Gypsy Verification Environment, which provides a set of tools for applying the methodology to the construction of programs. The programmer writes the specifications and the code itself; the system keeps track of the various aspects of the software (specifications, code and proof) and helps out in proving most theorems. When this book went to press, Gypsy had been used to develop two substantial programs: a "message flow modulator" that filters out illegal messages in the flow from one machine to another (556 executable lines of code) and an interface to a computer network (4211 lines of code that are executed in parallel on two computers). Both programs have been extensively tested, and the process found no bugs.

Those facts must be understood in context. First, only the smaller program was proved "totally correct". The verification of the larger showed only that it had certain properties (such as never passing along an inappropriate message). That program might still fail in some other way, but the proof shows that certain mistakes won't be made. The second piece of bad news is the cost: the productivity was only a few lines of code per programmer per day (two on the small program, four on the large program). Further research should increase the productivity, but even this high a cost may be acceptable in high-security or life-critical applications. I'm optimistic about the promise of program verification for such applications; to learn more about Gypsy, see Good's "Mechanical proofs about computer programs" in *Phil. Trans. R. Soc. London* A 312, pp. 389-409 (1984).

PART II: **PERFORMANCE**

A simple, powerful program that delights its users and does not vex its builders — that is the programmer's ultimate goal and the emphasis of the four previous columns.

We'll turn our attention now to one specific aspect of delightful programs: efficiency. Inefficient programs sadden their users with late output and big bills. These columns therefore describe several paths to performance.

The next column surveys the approaches and how they interact. The three subsequent columns discuss three methods for improving run time, in the order in which they are usually applied:

Column 6 shows how "back-of-the-envelope" calculations used early in the design process can ensure that the basic system structure is efficient enough

Column 7 is about algorithm design techniques that sometimes dramatically reduce the run time of a module.

Column 8 discusses code tuning, which is usually done late in the implementation of a system.

To wrap up Part II, Column 9 turns to another aspect of performance: space efficiency.

There are two good reasons for studying efficiency. The first is its intrinsic importance in many applications. A software manager I know estimates that half his development budget goes to efficiency; a manager of a data processing installation has to purchase million-dollar mainframes to solve his performance problems. Many systems demand execution speed, including real-time programs, huge databases and machines dedicated to a single program.

The second reason for studying performance is educational. Apart from practical benefits, efficiency is a fine training ground. These columns cover ideas ranging from the theory of algorithms to common sense like "back-of-the-envelope" calculations. The major theme is fluidity of thinking; Column 5, especially, encourages us to look at a problem from many different viewpoints.

49

Similar lessons come from many other topics. These columns might have been built around user interfaces, system robustness, security, or accuracy of answers. Efficiency has the advantage that it can be measured: we can all agree that one program is 2.5 times faster than another, while discussions on user interfaces, for instance, often get bogged down in personal tastes.

Column 5 appeared in the November 1984 *Communications of the ACM*, Column 6 in March, Column 7 in September, Column 8 in February, and Column 9 in May.

COLUMN 5: **PERSPECTIVE ON PERFORMANCE**

The next three columns describe three different approaches to run-time efficiency. In this column we'll see how those parts fit together into a whole: each technique is applicable to one of several *design levels* at which computer systems are built. We'll first study one particular program, and then turn to a more systematic view of design levels.

5.1 A Case Study

Andrew Appel describes "An efficient program for many-body simulations" in the January 1985 *SIAM Journal on Scientific and Statistical Computing 6*, 1, pp. 85-103. By working on the program at several levels, he reduced its run time from a year to a day.

The program solves the classical "N-body problem" of computing interactions in a gravitational field. It simulates the motions of N objects in 3-space, given their masses and initial positions and velocities; think of the objects as planets, stars or galaxies. In two dimensions, the input might look like

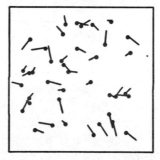

Appel's paper describes two astrophysical problems in which $N=10,000$; by studying simulation runs, physicists can test how well a theory matches astronomical observations.

The obvious simulation program divides time into small "steps" and computes the progress of each object at each step. Because it computes the attraction of each object to every other, the cost per time step is proportional to N^2. Appel estimated that 1,000 time steps of such an algorithm with $N = 10,000$ would require roughly one year on a VAX-11/780 or one day on a Cray-1.

The final program solves the problem in less than a day on a VAX-11/780 (for a speedup factor of 400) and has been used by several physicists. The following brief survey of his program will ignore many important details that can be found in his paper; the important message is that a huge speedup was achieved by working at several different levels.

Algorithms and Data Structures. Appel's first priority was to reduce the $O(N^2)$ cost per time step to $O(N \log N)$.† He therefore represents the physical objects as leaves in a binary tree; higher nodes represent clusters of objects. The force operating on a particular object can be approximated by the force exerted by the large clusters; Appel showed that this approximation does not bias the simulation. The tree has roughly $\log N$ levels, and the resulting $O(N \log N)$ algorithm is similar in spirit to the algorithm in Section 7.3. This change reduced the run time of the program by a factor of 12.

Algorithm Tuning. The simple algorithm always uses small time steps to handle the rare case that two particles come close to one another. The tree data structure allows such pairs to be recognized and handled by a special procedure. That doubles the time step size and thereby halves the run time of the program.

Data Structure Reorganization. The tree that represents the initial set of objects is quite poor at representing later sets. Reconfiguring the data structure at each time step costs a little time, but reduces the number of local calculations and thereby halves the total run time.

Code Tuning. Due to additional numerical accuracy provided by the tree, 64-bit double-precision floating point numbers could be replaced by 32-bit single-precision numbers; that change halved the run time. Profiling the program showed that 98 percent of the run time was spent in one procedure; rewriting that code in assembly language increased its speed by a factor of 2.5.

Hardware. After all the above changes, the program still required two days of VAX-11/780 run time, and several runs of the program were desired. Appel therefore transported the program to a similar machine equipped with a floating point accelerator, which halved its run time.

The changes described above multiply together for a total speedup factor of

---

† The notation $O(N^2)$ can be thought of as "proportional to N^2"; both $15N^2 + 100N$ and $N^2/2 - 10$ are $O(N^2)$. Informally, $f(N) = O(g(N))$ means that $f(N) < cg(N)$ for some constant c and sufficiently large values of N. A formal definition of the notation can be found in most textbooks on algorithm design or discrete mathematics, and Section 7.5 illustrates the relevance of the notation to program design.

400; Appel's final program runs a 10,000-body simulation in about one day. The speedups were not free, though. The simple algorithm may be expressed in a few dozen lines of code, while the fast program required 1200 lines of Pascal. The design and implementation of the fast program required several months of Appel's time. The speedups are summarized in the following table.

Design Level	Speedup Factor	Modification
Algorithms and Data Structures	12	A binary tree reduces $O(N^2)$ time to $O(N \log N)$
Algorithm Tuning	2	Use larger time steps
Data Structure Reorganization	2	Produce clusters well-suited to the tree algorithm
System-Independent Code Tuning	2	Replace double-precision floating point with single precision
System-Dependent Code Tuning	2.5	Recode the critical procedure in assembly language
Hardware	2	Use a floating point accelerator
Total	400	

This table illustrates several kinds of dependence among speedups. The primary speedup is the tree data structure, which opened the door for the next three changes. The last two speedups, changing to assembly code and using the floating point accelerator, were in this case independent of the tree. The tree structure would have less of an impact on a Cray-1 (whose pipelined architecture is well-suited to the simple algorithm), so we see that algorithmic speedups are not necessarily independent of hardware.

5.2 Design Levels

A computer system is designed at many levels, ranging from its high-level software structure down to the transistors in its hardware. The following survey is intended only as an intuitive guide to design levels, so don't expect a formal taxonomy.

Problem Definition. The battle for a fast system can be won or lost in specifying the problem it is to solve. On the day I wrote this paragraph, a vendor told me that he couldn't deliver supplies because a purchase order had been lost somewhere between my organization and my company's purchasing department. Purchasing was swamped with similar orders; fifty people in my organization alone had placed individual orders. A friendly chat between my management and purchasing resulted in consolidating those fifty orders into one large order. In addition to easing administrative work for both organizations, this change sped up one small part of a computer system by a factor of fifty. A good systems analyst keeps an eye out for such savings, both before and after systems are deployed.

Sometimes good specifications give users a little less than what they thought was needed. In Column 1 we saw how incorporating a few important facts about the input to a sorting program decreased both its run time and its code length by an order of magnitude. Problem specification can have a subtle interaction with efficiency; for example, good error-recovery may make a compiler slightly slower, but it usually decreases its overall time by reducing the number of compilations.

System Structure. The decomposition of a large system into modules is probably the single most important factor in determining its performance. Here are two distinct organizations for a query-answering system.

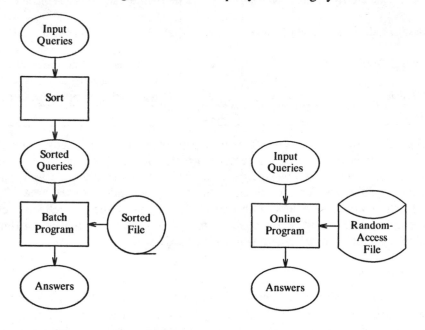

Figure 1. Two system structures.

These structures are two canonical ways of bringing together related information; they also arise in file updating programs and spelling checkers (we'll return to these structures in Column 13). Problem 1 shows that each organization is fast in some contexts and slow in others. After decomposing a system into modules, the designer should do a simple "back-of-the-envelope" estimate to make sure that its performance is in the right ballpark; such calculations are the subject of Column 6. Because efficiency is much easier to build into a new system than to retrofit into an existing system, performance analysis is crucial during system design.

Algorithms and Data Structures. The keys to a fast module are usually the structures that represent its data and the algorithms that operate on the data. The largest single improvement in Appel's program came from replacing an $O(N^2)$ algorithm with an $O(N \log N)$ algorithm; Columns 2 and 7 describe similar speedups.

Code Tuning. Appel achieved a factor of five by making small changes to code; Column 8 is devoted to that topic.

System Software. Sometimes it's easier to change the software on which a system is built than the system itself. Section 6.4, for instance, describes how replacing an interpreted language with a compiled language could increase performance by a factor of several hundred. Other available speedups include compiler optimizations (including a language's run-time system) and operating system and database system modifications.

Hardware. There are many ways that faster hardware can increase performance. General-purpose computers are sometimes fast enough; speedups are available through faster implementations of the same architecture, multiprocessors, and supercomputers. Sometimes it is more cost-effective to build a special-purpose box that handles just the particular problem at hand; special-purpose chips for speech synthesis, for example, enable inexpensive toys and household appliances to talk. Appel's solution of adding a floating point accelerator to the existing machine was somewhere between the two extremes.

5.3 Principles

Because an ounce of prevention is worth a pound of cure, we should keep in mind an observation due to Gordon Bell of Encore Computer Corporation.

> *The cheapest, fastest and most reliable components of a computer system are those that aren't there.*

Those missing components are also the most accurate (they never make mistakes), the most secure (they can't be broken into), and the easiest to design, document, test and maintain. The importance of a simple design can't be overemphasized.

But when performance problems can't be sidestepped, thinking about design levels can help focus a programmer's effort.

If you need a little speedup, work at the best level. Most programmers have their own knee-jerk response to efficiency: "change algorithms" or "tune the queueing discipline" spring quickly to some lips. Before you decide to work at any given level, consider all possible levels and choose the one that delivers the most speedup for the least effort.

If you need a big speedup, work at many levels. Enormous speedups like Appel's are achieved only by attacking a problem on several different fronts, and they usually take a great deal of effort. When changes on one level are independent of changes on other levels (as they often, but not always, are), the various speedups multiply.

Columns 6, 7 and 8 discuss speedups at three different design levels; keep perspective as you consider the individual speedups.

5.4 Problems

1. Figure 1 in Section 5.2 shows two possible organizations for a simple query-answering system. Assume that each of the one million records in the file is identified by a key and that each query refers (by key) to a single record. Further assume that both files are stored on disk in 100-record blocks, and that a random block can be read from disk in 50 milliseconds while blocks can be read sequentially every 5 milliseconds. The batch program reads the entire file, while the online algorithm reads only relevant blocks but may read some blocks many times. When is the batch method more efficient than the online program?

2. Discuss speedups at various design levels for some of the following problems: simulating Conway's "Game of Life", factoring 100-digit integers, Fourier analysis, simulating VLSI chips, and searching a large text file on disk for a given string. Discuss the dependencies of the proposed speedups.

3. Appel found that changing from double-precision arithmetic to single-precision arithmetic doubled the speed of his program. Choose an appropriate test and measure that speedup on your system.

4. This column concentrates on run-time efficiency. Other common measures of performance include fault-tolerance, reliability, security, cost, cost/performance ratio, accuracy, and robustness to user error. Discuss how each of these problems can be attacked at several design levels.

5. Discuss the costs of employing state-of-the-art technologies at the various design levels. Include all relevant measures of cost, including development time (calendar and personnel), maintainability, and dollar cost.

6. An old and popular saying claims that "efficiency is secondary to correctness — a program's speed is immaterial if its answers are wrong". True or false?

7. Discuss different solutions to problems in everyday life, such as injuries suffered in automobile accidents.

5.5 Further Reading

I learned the theme of this column from Raj Reddy and Allen Newell's paper "Multiplicative speedup of systems" (in *Perspectives on Computer Science*, edited by A. K. Jones and published in 1977 by Academic Press). Their work was motivated by problems in Artificial Intelligence; they conjecture that speech and vision systems might be sped up by a factor of a million. Their paper describes speedups at various design levels, and is especially rich in speedups due to hardware and system software.

Butler Lampson's "Hints for Computer System Design" appears in *IEEE Software 1*, 1, January 1984. Many of the hints deal with performance; his paper is particularly strong at integrated hardware/software system design.

COLUMN 6: **THE BACK OF THE ENVELOPE**

It was in the middle of a fascinating conversation on software engineering that Bob Martin asked me, "How much water flows out of the Mississippi River in a day?" Because I had found his comments up to that point deeply insightful, I politely stifled my true response and said, "Pardon me?" When he asked again I realized that I had no choice but to humor the poor fellow, who had obviously cracked under the pressures of running a large software shop within Bell Labs.

My response went something like this. I figured that near its mouth the river was about a mile wide and maybe twenty feet deep (or about one two-hundred-and-fiftieth of a mile). I guessed that the rate of flow was five miles an hour, or a hundred and twenty miles per day. Multiplying

$$1 \text{ mile} \times 1/250 \text{ mile} \times 120 \text{ miles/day} \approx 1/2 \text{ mile}^3/\text{day}$$

showed that the river discharged about half a cubic mile of water per day, to within an order of magnitude. But so what?

At that point Martin picked up from his desk a proposal for the computer-based mail system that AT&T developed for the 1984 Summer Olympic games, and went through a similar sequence of calculations. Although his numbers were straight from the proposal and therefore more precise, the calculations were just as simple and much more revealing. They showed that, under generous assumptions, the proposed system could work only if there were at least a hundred and twenty seconds in each minute. He had sent the design back to the drawing board the previous day. (The conversation took place in early 1983, and the final system was used during the Olympics without a hitch.)

That was Bob Martin's wonderful (if eccentric) way of introducing the engineering technique of "back-of-the-envelope" calculations. The idea is standard fare in engineering schools and is bread and butter for most practicing engineers. Unfortunately, it is too often neglected in computing.

59

6.1 Basic Skills

These basic reminders can be quite helpful in making back-of-the-envelope calculations.

Two Answers Are Better Than One. When I asked Peter Weinberger how much water flows out of the Mississippi per day, he responded, "As much as flows in." He then estimated that the Mississippi basin was about 1000 by 1000 miles, and that the annual runoff from rainfall there was about one foot (or one five-thousandth of a mile). That gives

$$1000 \text{ miles} \times 1000 \text{ miles} \times 1/5000 \text{ mile/year} \approx 200 \text{ miles}^3/\text{year}$$

$$200 \text{ miles}^3/\text{year} \ / \ 400 \text{ days/year} \approx 1/2 \text{ mile}^3/\text{day}$$

or a little more than half a cubic mile per day. It's important to double check all calculations, and especially so for quick ones.

As a cheating triple check, an almanac reported that the river's discharge is 640,000 cubic feet per second. Working from that gives

$$640,000 \text{ ft}^3/\text{sec} \times 3600 \text{ secs/hr} \approx 2.3 \times 10^9 \text{ ft}^3/\text{hr}$$

$$2.3 \times 10^9 \text{ ft}^3/\text{hr} \times 24 \text{ hrs/day} \approx 6 \times 10^{10} \text{ ft}^3/\text{day}$$

$$6 \times 10^{10} \text{ ft}^3/\text{day} \ / \ (5000 \text{ ft/mile})^3 \approx 6 \times 10^{10} \text{ ft}^3/\text{day} \ / \ (125 \times 10^9 \text{ ft}^3/\text{mile}^3)$$

$$\approx 60/125 \text{ mile}^3/\text{day}$$

$$\approx 1/2 \text{ mile}^3/\text{day}$$

The proximity of the two estimates to one another, and especially to the almanac's answer, is a fine example of sheer dumb luck.

Quick Checks. Polya devotes three pages of his *How To Solve It* to "Test by Dimension", which he describes as a "well-known, quick and efficient means to check geometrical or physical formulas". The first rule is that the dimensions in a sum must be the same, which is in turn the dimension of the sum — you can add feet together to get feet, but you can't add seconds to pounds. The second rule is that the dimension of a product is the product of the dimensions. The examples above obey both rules; multiplying

$$(\text{miles}+\text{miles}) \times \text{miles} \times \text{miles/day} = \text{miles}^3/\text{day}$$

has the right form, apart from any constants.

A simple table can help you keep track of dimensions in complicated expressions like those above. To perform Weinberger's calculation, we first write down the three original factors.

1000	miles	1000	miles	1	mile
				5000	year

Next we simplify the expression by cancelling terms, which shows that the output is 200 miles^3/year.

1000 miles	1000 miles	1 mile	200	mile^3
		5000 year		

Now we multiply by the identity (well, almost) that there are 400 days per year.

1000 miles	1000 miles	1 mile	200	mile^3		year
		5000 year			400	days

Cancellation yields the (by now familiar) answer of half a cubic mile per day.

1000 miles	1000 miles	1 mile	200	mile^3		year	1
		5000 year			400	days	2

These tabular calculations help you keep track of dimensions.

Dimension tests check the form of equations. Check your multiplications and divisions with an old trick from slide rule days: independently compute the leading digit and the exponent. There are several quick checks for addition.

```
  3142            3142            3142
  2718            2718            2718
+1123           +1123           +1123
 ----            ----            ----
  983            6982            6973
```

The first sum has too few digits and the second errs in the least significant digit. "Casting out nines" reveals the error in the third example: the digits in the summands sum to 8 modulo 9, while those in the answer sum to 7 modulo 9 (in a correct addition, the sums of the digits are equal after "casting out" groups of digits that sum to nine).

Above all, don't forget common sense: be suspicious of any calculations that show that the Mississippi River discharges 100 gallons of water per day.

6.2 Quick Calculations in Computing

Card, Moran and Newell paint an ambitious picture of estimation on pages 9 and 10 of their *Psychology of Human-Computer Interaction* (published by Erlbaum in 1983).

A system designer, the head of a small team writing the specifications for a desktop calendar-scheduling system, is choosing between having users type a key for each command and having them point to a menu with a lightpen. On his whiteboard, he lists some representative tasks users of his system must perform. In two columns, he writes the steps needed by the "key-command" and "menu" options. From a handbook, he culls the times for each step, adding the step times to get total task times. The key-command system takes less time, but only slightly. But, applying the analysis from another section of the handbook, he calculates that the menu system will be faster to learn; in fact, it will be learnable in half the time. He has estimated previously that an effective menu system will require a more expensive processor: 20% more memory, 100% more microcode memory, and a more expensive display. Is the extra expenditure worthwhile? A few more minutes of calculation and he realizes the startling fact that, for the manufacturing quantities now anticipated, training costs for the key-command system will exceed unit manufacturing costs! The increase in hardware costs would be much more than balanced by the decrease in training costs, even before considering the increase in market that can be expected for a more easily learned system. Are there advantages to the key-command system in other areas, which need to be balanced? He proceeds with other analyses, considering the load on the user's memory, the potential for user errors, and the likelihood of fatigue. In the next room, the Pascal compiler hums idly, unused, awaiting his decision.

Their book then goes on to develop a scientific base in psychology that is a necessary precursor to such a handbook.

That scenario shows how a few envelopes' worth of arithmetic might enable a system designer to make a rational choice between two appealing alternatives. That is a fundamentally different use than Martin's calculation for the Olympic mail system: his analysis of a single design uncovered a fatal flaw (similar calculations in Section 2.4 showed the folly of simple anagram algorithms). In both cases, a short sequence of calculations was sufficient to answer the question at hand; additional figuring would have shed little light.

Early in the life of a system, rapid calculations can steer the designer away from dangerous waters into safe passages. And if you don't use them early, they may show in retrospect that a project was doomed to failure. The calculations are often trivial, employing no more than high school mathematics. The hard part is remembering to use them soon enough.

6.3 Safety Factors

The output of any calculation is only as good as its input. With good data, simple calculations can yield accurate answers which are sometimes quite useful. In 1969 Don Knuth wrote a disk sorting package, only to find that it took twice the time predicted by his calculations. Diligent checking uncovered the flaw: due to a software bug, the system's one-year-old disks had run at only half their advertised speed for their entire lives. When the bug was fixed, the sorting package behaved as predicted and every other disk-bound program also ran faster.

Often, though, sloppy input is enough to get into the right ballpark. If you guess about twenty percent here and fifty percent there and still find that a design is a hundred times above or below specification, additional accuracy isn't needed. But before placing too much confidence in a twenty percent margin of error, consider Vic Vyssotsky's advice from a talk he has given on several occasions.

"Most of you", says Vyssotsky, "probably recall pictures of 'Galloping Gertie', the Tacoma Narrows bridge which tore itself apart in a windstorm in 1940.† Well, suspension bridges had been ripping themselves apart that way for eighty years or so before Galloping Gertie. It's an aerodynamic lift phenomenon, and to do a proper engineering calculation of the forces, which involve drastic nonlinearities, you have to use the mathematics and concepts of Kolmogorov to model the eddy spectrum. Nobody really knew how to do this correctly in detail until the 1950's or thereabouts. So, why hasn't the Brooklyn Bridge torn itself apart, like Galloping Gertie?

"It's because John Roebling had sense enough to know what he *didn't* know. His notes and letters on the design of the Brooklyn Bridge still exist, and they are a fascinating example of a good engineer recognizing the limits of his knowledge. He knew about aerodynamic lift on suspension bridges; he had watched it. And he knew he didn't know enough to model it. So he designed the stiffness of the truss on the Brooklyn Bridge roadway to be *six times* what a normal calculation based on known static and dynamic loads would have called for. And, he specified a network of diagonal stays running down to the roadway, to stiffen the entire bridge structure. Go look at those sometime; they're almost unique.

"When Roebling was asked whether his proposed bridge wouldn't collapse like so many others, he said, 'No, because I designed it six times as strong as it needs to be, to prevent that from happening.'

"Roebling was a good engineer, and he built a good bridge, by employing a huge safety factor to compensate for his ignorance. Do we do that? I submit to you that in calculating performance of our real-time software systems we ought to derate them by a factor of two, or four, or six, to compensate for our ignorance. In making reliability/availability commitments, we ought to stay back from the objectives we *think* we can meet by a factor of ten, to compensate for our ignorance. In estimating size and cost and schedule, we should be conservative by a factor of two or four to compensate for our ignorance. We should design the way John Roebling did, and not the way his contemporaries did — so far as I know, none of the suspension bridges built by Roebling's

---

† For more information on the event, see Section 2.6.1 of Braun's *Differential Equations and Their Applications*, Second Edition, published in 1978 by Springer-Verlag.

contemporaries in the United States still stands, and a quarter of all the bridges of any type built in the U.S. in the 1870's collapsed within ten years of their construction.

"Are we engineers, like John Roebling? I wonder."

6.4 A Case Study

To make the above points more concrete, I'll describe how I (almost) used them in a system I built for a small company in early 1982. The details can be found in Carnegie-Mellon University Computer Science Technical Report CMU-CS-83-108; I'll just sketch them here.

The system prepared several reports a day to summarize the data on one thousand eighty-column records; the reports were each about eighty pages long. The system's predecessor ran on a large mainframe; my task was to implement a similar system on a personal computer, using interpreted BASIC.

Early in the design of the system I did simple calculations to make sure that the personal computer was up to this application. The space analysis was simple: I calculated the size of the several largest tables and found that they used only half of the 48K bytes of the machine. The time analysis was centered around two main phases.

I didn't worry much about the time for Phase 1: a previous system did that task on an IBM System/360 Model 25 in a minute, and the microprocessor on the personal computer was more powerful than that old workhorse. Instead, I concentrated on Phase 2, which I thought would be limited by the sixty-lines-per-minute speed of the printer. Each page of the report contained about thirty lines, so the total time of forty minutes was well within bounds. After this short analysis, the company purchased three personal computers and I implemented the design.

The first implementation of the program was revealing. Storing the BASIC program required about twenty kilobytes of main memory that I had ignored in my calculation; the safety factor of two saved the day. The forty minutes of printing time was right on the mark. Unfortunately, I was way off in the time to read the records and build the table. Instead of taking a minute, it took *fourteen hours*, which made it awfully hard to prepare a few reports a day. The problem was that I had compared assembly code on the old System/360 with interpreted BASIC on the personal computer, ignoring the fact that interpreted BASIC usually runs several hundred times slower than assembly code.

At that point I did a more careful back-of-the-envelope calculation. Using the parameters described above (1000 records of 80 columns each) and ballpark guesses at other parameters (50 BASIC instructions per column and one hundred BASIC instructions per second) gave the following.

$$\frac{1000 \quad \text{recs}}{} \left| \begin{array}{c} 80 \quad \text{cols} \\ \text{rec} \end{array} \right| \begin{array}{c} 50 \quad \text{insts} \\ \text{col} \end{array} \left| \begin{array}{c} 1 \quad \text{sec} \\ 100 \quad \text{insts} \end{array} \right.$$

Multiplying and cancelling shows that the job takes

$$\frac{\cancel{1000} \quad \cancel{\text{recs}}}{} \left| \begin{array}{c} \cancel{80} \quad \cancel{\text{cols}} \\ \cancel{\text{rec}} \end{array} \right| \begin{array}{c} \cancel{50} \quad \cancel{\text{insts}} \\ \cancel{\text{col}} \end{array} \left| \begin{array}{c} \cancel{1} \quad \text{sec} \\ \cancel{100} \quad \cancel{\text{insts}} \end{array} \right| 40000$$

or 40,000 seconds. Dividing by the identity 3600 secs/hr gives the estimate of about eleven hours. Alternatively, I knew that the old machine took one minute for the task and executed an instruction in about ten microseconds. The slowdown to ten milliseconds is a factor of one thousand, and one thousand times the previous value of one minute is about seventeen hours.

Had I known the expense of this approach before I built the program, I would have used a faster language. Instead, I had an existing 600-line program and no choice but to tune the code, using the techniques of Column 8. The 70 lines of code in Phase 1 accounted for over 90 percent of the run time, and just 3 lines accounted for 11 hours (less than one percent of the code took 75 percent of the time!). I spent forty hours replacing 70 lines of BASIC with 110 lines of BASIC and 30 lines of assembly code; that reduced the time of Phase 1 from fourteen hours to two hours and twenty minutes. That was good enough for this particular system, but more than it might have been had I done a quick calculation beforehand and then chosen a more efficient implementation language.

6.5 Principles

When you use back-of-the-envelope calculations, be sure to recall Einstein's famous advice.

Everything should be made as simple as possible, but no simpler.

We know that simple calculations aren't too simple by including safety factors to compensate for our mistakes in estimating parameters and our ignorance of the problem at hand.

6.6 Problems

1. At what distances can a courier on a bicycle with a reel of magnetic tape be a more rapid carrier of information than a telephone line that transmits 56,000 bits per second? Than a 1200-bps line?
2. How long would it take you to fill a disk by typing?

3. When is it cost-effective to supply a programmer with a home terminal?

4. Suppose the world is slowed down by a factor of a million. How long does it take for your computer to execute an instruction? Your disk to rotate once? Your disk arm to seek across the disk? You to type your name?

5. Which has the most computational oomph: a second of supercomputer time, a minute of midicomputer time, an hour of microcomputer time, or a day of BASIC on a personal computer?

6. Suppose that a system makes 100 disk accesses to process a transaction (although some systems need fewer, some systems require several hundred disk accesses per transaction). How many transactions per hour per disk can the system handle?

7. A programmer spends one calendar day and one hour of CPU time to speed up a program by ten percent on a machine that costs one hundred dollars per hour of CPU time. Individual runs of the program typically require a minute of CPU time. How long will it take to pay for the speedup if the program is run a hundred times a day? What if the speedup were a factor of two or a factor of ten?

8. [R. Pike] Many compilers have optimizers that, when enabled, produce more efficient code. If your compiler has such an option, measure how much more compile time it takes and how much faster the resulting object code is. When is it worthwhile to run your optimizer? When is it worthwhile to build such an optimizer?

9. I was once asked to write a program to transmit data from one personal computer to another PC of a very different architecture. Since the file had only 400 records of 20 numeric digits each, I suggested re-keying the data from a readily available listing. Estimate costs associated with each approach, including programmer time, hardware investment, and transmission cost.

10. An article on page 652 of the July 1984 *Communications of the ACM* states that "the system handles an average of 7,328,764 transactions a day". Any comments?

11. Use quick calculations to estimate the run time of designs described in this book.

   a. Evaluate the designs in Problems 1.7, 2.7 and 5.1 and in Sections 2.2, 2.4, 5.2, 13.1 and 13.3.

   b. "Big-oh" arithmetic can be viewed as a formalization of quick calculations — it captures the growth rate but ignores constant factors. Use the "big-oh" run times of the algorithms in Columns 5, 7, 10, 11 and 12 to estimate the run time of their implementation as programs. Compare your estimates to the experiments reported in the columns.

6.7 Further Reading

Douglas Hofstadter's "Metamagical Themas" column in the May 1982 *Scientific American* is subtitled "Number numbness, or why innumeracy may be just as dangerous as illiteracy"; it is reprinted with a postscript in his book *Metamagical Themas*, published by Basic Books in 1985. It is a fine introduction to ballpark estimates and an eloquent statement of their importance.

Physicists are well aware of this topic. After this column appeared in *Communications of the ACM*, Jan Wolitzky wrote

> I've often heard "back-of-the-envelope" calculations referred to as "Fermi approximations", after the physicist. The story is that Enrico Fermi, Robert Oppenheimer, and the other Manhattan Project brass were behind a low blast wall awaiting the detonation of the first nuclear device from a few thousand yards away. Fermi was tearing up sheets of paper into little pieces, which he tossed into the air when he saw the flash. After the shock wave passed, he paced off the distance travelled by the paper shreds, performed a quick "back-of-the-envelope" calculation, and arrived at a figure for the explosive yield of the bomb, which was confirmed much later by expensive monitoring equipment.

Edward Purcell edits a monthly column in the *American Journal of Physics* entitled "The Back of the Envelope". It is full of such delightful questions as "A 60-watt bulb lit for a year takes how many barrels of oil?" and "How long would it take to transmit over a video channel the information contained in the human genome, approximately 1 meter of DNA?"

6.8 Quick Calculations in Everyday Life *[Sidebar]*

The publication of this column in *Communications of the ACM* provoked many interesting letters. One reader told of hearing an advertisement state that a salesperson had driven a new car 100,000 miles in one year, and then asking his son to examine the validity of the claim. Here's one quick answer: there are 2000 working hours per year (50 weeks times 40 hours per week), and a salesperson might average 50 miles per hour; that ignores time spent actually selling, but it does multiply to the claim. The statement is therefore at the outer limits of believability.

Everyday life presents us with many opportunities to hone our skills at quick calculations. For instance, how much money have you spent in the past year eating in restaurants? I was once horrified to hear a New Yorker quickly compute that he and his wife spend more money each month on taxicabs than they spend on rent. And for California readers (who may not know what a taxicab is), how long does it take to fill a swimming pool with a garden hose?

Several readers commented that quick calculations are appropriately taught at an early age. Roger Pinkham of the Stevens Institute of Technology wrote

> I am a teacher and have tried for years to teach "back-of-the-envelope" calculations to anyone who would listen. I have been marvelously unsuccessful. It seems to require a doubting-Thomas turn of mind.
>
> My father beat it into me. I come from the coast of Maine, and as a small child I was privy to a conversation between my father and his friend Homer Potter. Homer maintained that two ladies from Connecticut were pulling 200 pounds of lobsters a day. My father said, "Let's see. If you pull a pot every fifteen minutes, and say you get three legal per pot, that's 12 an hour or about 100 per day. I don't believe it!"
>
> "Well it is true!" swore Homer. "You never believe anything!"
>
> Father wouldn't believe it, and that was that. Two weeks later Homer said, "You know those two ladies, Fred? They were only pulling 20 pounds a day."
>
> Gracious to a fault, father grunted, "Now that I believe."

Several other readers discussed teaching this attitude to children, from the viewpoints of both parent and child. Popular questions were of the form "How long would it take you to walk to Washington, D.C.?" and "How many leaves did we rake this year?" Administered properly, such questions seem to encourage a life-long inquisitiveness in children, at the cost of bugging the heck out of the poor kids at the time.

COLUMN 7: ALGORITHM DESIGN TECHNIQUES

Column 2 describes the "everyday" impact that algorithm design can have on programmers: an algorithmic view of a problem gives insights that can make a program simpler to understand and to write. In this column we'll study a contribution of the field that is less frequent but more impressive: sophisticated algorithmic methods sometimes lead to dramatic performance improvements.

This column is built around one small problem, with an emphasis on the algorithms that solve it and the techniques used to design the algorithms. Some of the algorithms are a little complicated, but with justification. While the first program we'll study takes thirty-nine days to solve a problem of size ten thousand, the final one solves the same problem in less than a second.

7.1 The Problem and a Simple Algorithm

The problem arose in one-dimensional pattern recognition; I'll describe its history later. The input is a vector X of N real numbers; the output is the maximum sum found in any *contiguous* subvector of the input. For instance, if the input vector is

then the program returns the sum of $X[3..7]$, or 187. The problem is easy when all the numbers are positive — the maximum subvector is the entire input vector. The rub comes when some of the numbers are negative: should we include a negative number in hopes that the positive numbers to its sides will compensate for its negative contribution? To complete the definition of the problem, we'll say that when all inputs are negative the maximum sum subvector is the empty vector, which has sum zero.

69

The obvious program for this task iterates over all pairs of integers L and U satisfying $1 \leq L \leq U \leq N$; for each pair it computes the sum of $X[L..U]$ and checks whether that sum is greater than the maximum sum so far. The pseudocode for Algorithm 1 is

```
MaxSoFar := 0.0
for L := 1 to N do
    for U := L to N do
        Sum := 0.0
        for I := L to U do
            Sum := Sum + X[I]
        /* Sum now contains the sum of X[L..U] */
        MaxSoFar := max(MaxSoFar, Sum)
```

This code is short, straightforward, and easy to understand. Unfortunately, it has the severe disadvantage of being slow. On the computer I typically use, for instance, the code takes about an hour if N is 1000 and thirty-nine days if N is 10,000; we'll get to timing details in Section 7.5.

Those times are anecdotal; we get a different kind of feeling for the algorithm's efficiency using the "big-oh" notation described in Section 5.1. The statements in the outermost loop are executed exactly N times, and those in the middle loop are executed at most N times in each execution of the outer loop. Multiplying those two factors of N shows that the four lines contained in the middle loop are executed $O(N^2)$ times. The loop in those four lines is never executed more than N times, so its cost is $O(N)$. Multiplying the cost per inner loop times its number of executions shows that the cost of the entire program is proportional to N cubed, so we'll refer to this as a cubic algorithm.

This example illustrates the technique of big-oh analysis of run time and many of its strengths and weaknesses. Its primary weakness is that we still don't really know the amount of time the program will take for any particular input; we just know that the number of steps it executes is $O(N^3)$. That weakness is often compensated for by two strong points of the method. Big-oh analyses are usually easy to perform (as above), and the asymptotic run time is often sufficient for a back-of-the-envelope calculation to decide whether or not a program is efficient enough for a given application.

The next several sections use asymptotic run time as the only measure of program efficiency. If that makes you uncomfortable, peek ahead to Section 7.5, which shows that for this problem such analyses are extremely informative. Before you read further, though, take a minute to try to find a faster algorithm.

7.2 Two Quadratic Algorithms

Most programmers have the same response to Algorithm 1: "There's an obvious way to make it a lot faster." There are two obvious ways, however, and if one is obvious to a given programmer then the other often isn't. Both algorithms are quadratic — they take $O(N^2)$ steps on an input of size N — and both achieve their run time by computing the sum of $X[L..U]$ in a constant number of steps rather than in the $U-L+1$ steps of Algorithm 1. But the two quadratic algorithms use very different methods to compute the sum in constant time.

The first quadratic algorithm computes the sum quickly by noticing that the sum of $X[L..U]$ has an intimate relationship to the sum previously computed, that of $X[L..U-1]$. Exploiting that relationship leads to Algorithm 2.

```
MaxSoFar := 0.0
for L := 1 to N do
    Sum := 0.0
    for U := L to N do
        Sum := Sum + X[U]
        /* Sum now contains the sum of X[L..U] */
        MaxSoFar := max(MaxSoFar, Sum)
```

The statements inside the first loop are executed N times, and those inside the second loop are executed at most N times on each execution of the outer loop, so the total run time is $O(N^2)$.

An alternative quadratic algorithm computes the sum in the inner loop by accessing a data structure built before the outer loop is ever executed. The Ith element of CumArray contains the cumulative sum of the values in $X[1..I]$, so the sum of the values in $X[L..U]$ can be found by computing $CumArray[U]-CumArray[L-1]$. This results in the following code for Algorithm 2b.

```
CumArray[0] := 0.0
for I := 1 to N do
    CumArray[I] := CumArray[I-1] + X[I]
MaxSoFar := 0.0
for L := 1 to N do
    for U := L to N do
        Sum := CumArray[U] - CumArray[L-1]
        /* Sum now contains the sum of X[L..U] */
        MaxSoFar := max(MaxSoFar, Sum)
```

This code takes $O(N^2)$ time; the analysis is exactly the same as the analysis of Algorithm 2.

The algorithms we've seen so far inspect all possible pairs of starting and ending values of subvectors and consider the sum of the numbers in that subvector. Because there are $O(N^2)$ subvectors, any algorithm that inspects all such values must take at least quadratic time. Can you think of a way to sidestep this problem and achieve an algorithm that runs in less time?

7.3 A Divide-and-Conquer Algorithm

Our first subquadratic algorithm is complicated; if you get bogged down in its details, you won't lose much by skipping to the next section. It is based on the following divide-and-conquer schema:

> *To solve a problem of size N, recursively solve two subproblems of size approximately N/2, and combine their solutions to yield a solution to the complete problem.*

In this case the original problem deals with a vector of size *N*, so the most natural way to divide it into subproblems is to create two subvectors of approximately equal size, which we'll call *A* and *B*.

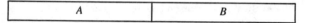

We then recursively find the maximum subvectors in *A* and *B*, which we'll call M_A and M_B.

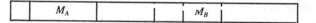

It is tempting to think that we have solved the problem because the maximum sum subvector of the entire vector must be either M_A or M_B, and that is almost right. In fact, the maximum is either entirely in *A*, entirely in *B*, or it crosses the border between *A* and *B*; we'll call that M_C for the maximum *crossing* the border.

Thus our divide-and-conquer algorithm will compute M_A and M_B recursively, compute M_C by some other means, and then return the maximum of the three.

That description is almost enough to write code. All we have left to describe is how we'll handle small vectors and how we'll compute M_C. The former is easy: the maximum of a one-element vector is the only value in the vector or zero if that number is negative, and the maximum of a zero-element vector was previously defined to be zero. To compute M_C we observe that its component in *A* is the largest subvector starting at the boundary and reaching into *A*, and similarly for its component in *B*. Putting these facts together leads to the following code for Algorithm 3, which is originally invoked by the procedure call

```
Answer := MaxSum(1,N)
```

```
recursive function MaxSum(L, U)
    if L > U then      /* Zero-element vector */
        return 0.0
    if L = U then      /* One-element vector */
        return max(0.0, X[L])

    M := (L+U)/2   /* A is X[L..M], B is X[M+1..U] */
    /* Find max crossing to left */
        Sum := 0.0; MaxToLeft := 0.0
        for I := M downto L do
            Sum := Sum + X[I]
            MaxToLeft := max(MaxToLeft, Sum)
    /* Find max crossing to right */
        Sum := 0.0; MaxToRight := 0.0
        for I := M+1 to U do
            Sum := Sum + X[I]
            MaxToRight := max(MaxToRight, Sum)
    MaxCrossing := MaxToLeft + MaxToRight

    MaxInA := MaxSum(L,M)
    MaxInB := MaxSum(M+1,U)
    return max(MaxCrossing, MaxInA, MaxInB)
```

The code is complicated and easy to get wrong, but it solves the problem in $O(N \log N)$ time. There are a number of ways to prove this fact. An informal argument observes that the algorithm does $O(N)$ work on each of $O(\log N)$ levels of recursion. The argument can be made more precise by the use of recurrence relations. If $T(N)$ denotes the time to solve a problem of size N, then $T(1)=O(1)$ and

$$T(N) = 2T(N/2) + O(N).$$

Problem 11 shows that this recurrence has the solution $T(N) = O(N \log N)$.

7.4 A Scanning Algorithm

We'll now use the simplest kind of algorithm that operates on arrays: it starts at the left end (element $X[1]$) and scans through to the right end (element $X[N]$), keeping track of the maximum sum subvector seen so far. The maximum is initially zero. Suppose that we've solved the problem for $X[1..I-1]$; how can we extend that to a solution for the first I elements? We use reasoning similar to that of the divide-and-conquer algorithm: the maximum sum in the first I elements is either the maximum sum in the first $I-1$ elements (which we'll call *MaxSoFar*), or it is that of a subvector that ends in position I (which we'll call *MaxEndingHere*).

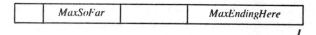

I

Recomputing *MaxEndingHere* from scratch using code like that in Algorithm 3 yields yet another quadratic algorithm. We can get around this by using the technique that led to Algorithm 2: instead of computing the maximum subvector ending in position *I* from scratch, we'll use the maximum subvector that ends in position $I-1$. This results in Algorithm 4.

```
MaxSoFar := 0.0
MaxEndingHere := 0.0
for I := 1 to N do
    /*  Invariant: MaxEndingHere and MaxSoFar
        are accurate for X[1..I-1] */
    MaxEndingHere := max(MaxEndingHere+X[I], 0.0)
    MaxSoFar := max(MaxSoFar, MaxEndingHere)
```

The key to understanding this program is the variable *MaxEndingHere*. Before the first assignment statement in the loop, *MaxEndingHere* contains the value of the maximum subvector ending in position $I-1$; the assignment statement modifies it to contain the value of the maximum subvector ending in position *I*. The statement increases it by the value $X[I]$ so long as doing so keeps it positive; when it goes negative, it is reset to zero because the maximum subvector ending at *I* is the empty vector. Although the code is subtle, it is short and fast: its run time is $O(N)$, so we'll refer to it as a linear algorithm. David Gries systematically derives and verifies this algorithm in his paper "A Note on the Standard Strategy for Developing Loop Invariants and Loops" in the journal *Science of Computer Programming 2*, pp. 207-214.

7.5 What Does It Matter?

So far I've played fast and loose with "big-ohs"; it's time for me to come clean and tell about the run times of the programs. I implemented the four primary algorithms (all except Algorithm 2b) in the C language on a VAX-11/750, timed them, and extrapolated the observed run times to achieve the following table.

ALGORITHM		1	2	3	4
Lines of C Code		8	7	14	7
Run time in microseconds		$3.4N^3$	$13N^2$	$46N \log_2 N$	$33N$
Time to solve a problem of size	10^2	3.4 secs	.13 secs	.03 secs	.003 secs
	10^3	.94 hrs	13 secs	.45 secs	.033 secs
	10^4	39 days	22 mins	6.1 secs	.33 secs
	10^5	108 yrs	1.5 days	1.3 mins	3.3 secs
	10^6	108 mill	5 mos	15 mins	33 secs
Max size problem solved in one	sec	67	280	2000	30,000
	min	260	2200	82,000	2,000,000
	hr	1000	17,000	3,500,000	120,000,000
	day	3000	81,000	73,000,000	2,800,000,000
If N multiplies by 10, time multiplies by		1000	100	10+	10
If time multiplies by 10, N multiplies by		2.15	3.16	10−	10

This table makes a number of points. The most important is that proper algorithm design can make a big difference in run time; that point is underscored by the middle rows. The last two rows show how increases in problem size are related to increases in run time.

Another important point is that when we're comparing cubic, quadratic, and linear algorithms with one another, the constant factors of the programs don't matter much. (The discussion of the $O(N!)$ algorithm in Section 2.4 shows that constant factors matter even less in functions that grow faster than polynomially.) To underscore this point, I conducted an experiment in which I tried to make the constant factors of two algorithms differ by as much as possible. To achieve a huge constant factor I implemented Algorithm 4 on a BASIC interpreter on a Radio Shack TRS-80 Model III microcomputer. For the other end of the spectrum, Eric Grosse and I implemented Algorithm 1 in fine-tuned FORTRAN on a Cray-1 supercomputer. We got the disparity we wanted: the run time of the cubic algorithm was measured as $3.0N^3$ nanoseconds, while the run time of the linear algorithm was $19.5N$ milliseconds, or $19,500,000N$ nanoseconds. This table shows how those expressions translate to times for various problem sizes.

N	CRAY-1, FORTRAN, CUBIC ALGORITHM	TRS-80, BASIC, LINEAR ALGORITHM
10	3.0 microsecs	200 millisecs
100	3.0 millisecs	2.0 secs
1000	3.0 secs	20 secs
10,000	49 mins	3.2 mins
100,000	35 days	32 mins
1,000,000	95 yrs	5.4 hrs

The difference in constant factors of six and a half million allowed the cubic algorithm to start off faster, but the linear algorithm was bound to catch up. The break-even point for the two algorithms is around 2,500, where each takes about fifty seconds.

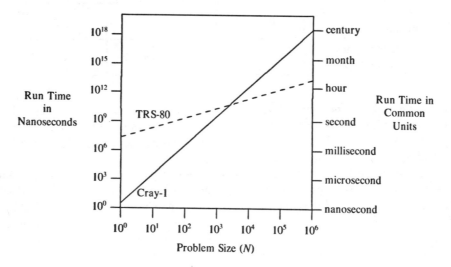

7.6 Principles

The history of the problem sheds light on the algorithm design techniques. The problem arose in a pattern-matching procedure designed by Ulf Grenander of Brown University in the two-dimensional form described in Problem 7. In that form, the maximum sum subarray was the maximum likelihood estimator of a certain kind of pattern in a digitized picture. Because the two-dimensional problem required too much time to solve, Grenander simplified it to one dimension to gain insight into its structure.

Grenander observed that the cubic time of Algorithm 1 was prohibitively slow, and derived Algorithm 2. In 1977 he described the problem to Michael Shamos of UNILOGIC, Ltd. (then of Carnegie-Mellon University) who overnight designed Algorithm 3. When Shamos showed me the problem shortly thereafter, we thought that it was probably the best possible; researchers had just shown that several similar problems require time proportional to $N \log N$. A few days later Shamos described the problem and its history at a Carnegie-Mellon seminar attended by statistician Jay Kadane, who designed Algorithm 4 within a minute. Fortunately, we know that there is no faster algorithm: any correct algorithm must take $O(N)$ time.

Even though the one-dimensional problem is completely solved, Grenander's original two-dimensional problem remained open eight years after it was posed, as this book went to press. Because of the computational expense of all known algorithms, Grenander had to abandon that approach to the pattern-matching problem. Readers who feel that the linear-time algorithm for the one-dimensional problem is "obvious" are therefore urged to find an "obvious" algorithm for Problem 7!

The algorithms in this story were never incorporated into a system, but they illustrate important algorithm design techniques that have had substantial impact on many systems (see Section 7.9).

Save state to avoid recomputation. This simple form of dynamic programming arose in Algorithms 2 and 4. By using space to store results, we avoid using time to recompute them.

Preprocess information into data structures. The *CumArray* structure in Algorithm 2b allowed the sum of a subvector to be computed in just a couple of operations.

Divide-and-conquer algorithms. Algorithm 3 uses a simple form of divide-and-conquer; textbooks on algorithm design describe more advanced forms.

Scanning algorithms. Problems on arrays can often be solved by asking "how can I extend a solution for $X[1..I-1]$ to a solution for $X[1..I]$?" Algorithm 4 stores both the old answer and some auxiliary data to compute the new answer.

Cumulatives. Algorithm 2b uses a cumulative table in which the Ith element contains the sum of the first I values of X; such tables are common when dealing with ranges. In business data processing applications, for instance, one finds the sales from March to October by subtracting the February year-to-date sales from the October year-to-date sales.

Lower bounds. Algorithm designers sleep peacefully only when they know their algorithms are the best possible; for this assurance, they must prove a matching lower bound. The linear lower bound for this problem is the subject of Problem 9; more complex lower bounds can be quite difficult.

7.7 Problems

1. Algorithms 3 and 4 use subtle code that is easy to get wrong. Use the program verification techniques of Column 4 to argue the correctness of the code; specify the loop invariants carefully.

2. Our analysis of the four algorithms was done only at the "big-oh" level of detail. Analyze the number of *max* functions used by each algorithm as exactly as possible; does this exercise give any insight into the running times of the programs? How much space does each algorithm require?

3. We defined the maximum subvector of an array of negative numbers to be zero, the sum of the empty subvector. Suppose that we had instead defined the maximum subvector to be the value of the largest element; how would you change the programs?

4. Suppose that we wished to find the subvector with the sum closest to zero rather than that with maximum sum. What is the most efficient algorithm you can design for this task? What algorithm design techniques are applicable? What if we wished to find the subvector with the sum closest to a given real number T?

5. A turnpike consists of $N-1$ stretches of road between N toll stations; each stretch has an associated cost of travel. It is trivial to tell the cost of going between any two stations in $O(N)$ time using only an array of the costs or in constant time using a table with $O(N^2)$ entries. Describe a data structure that requires $O(N)$ space but allows the cost of any route to be computed in constant time.

6. After the array $X[1..N]$ is initialized to zero, N of the following operations are performed

   ```
   for I := L to U do
       X[I] := X[I] + V
   ```

   where L, U and V are parameters of each operation (L and U are integers satisfying $1 \le L \le U \le N$ and V is a real). After the N operations, the values of $X[1]$ through $X[N]$ are reported in order. The method just sketched requires $O(N^2)$ time. Can you find a faster algorithm?

7. In the maximum subarray problem we are given an $N \times N$ array of reals, and we must find the maximum sum contained in any rectangular subarray. What is the complexity of this problem?

8. Modify Algorithm 3 (the divide-and-conquer algorithm) to run in linear worst-case time.

9. Prove that any correct algorithm for computing maximum subvectors must inspect all N inputs. (Algorithms for some problems may correctly ignore some inputs; consider Saxe's algorithm in Solution 2.2 and Boyer and Moore's substring searching algorithm in the October 1977 *CACM*.)

10. Given integers M and N and the real vector $X[1..N]$, find the integer I ($1 \le I \le N - M$) such that the sum $X[I] + ... + X[I + M]$ is nearest zero.

11. What is the solution of the recurrence $T(N) = 2T(N/2) + CN$ when $T(1) = 0$ and N is a power of two? Prove your result by mathematical induction. What if $T(1) = C$?

7.8 Further Reading

Only extensive study can put algorithm design techniques at your fingertips; most programmers will get this only from a textbook on algorithms. *Data Structures and Algorithms* by Aho, Hopcroft and Ullman (published by Addison-Wesley in 1983) is an excellent undergraduate text. Chapter 10 on "Algorithm Design Techniques" is especially relevant to this column.

7.9 The Impact of Algorithms *[Sidebar]*

Although the problem studied in this column illustrates several important techniques, it's really a toy — it was never incorporated into a system. We'll now survey a few real problems in which algorithm design techniques proved their worth.

Numerical Analysis. The standard example of the power of algorithm design is the discrete Fast Fourier Transform (FFT). Its divide and conquer structure reduced the time required for Fourier analysis from $O(N^2)$ to $O(N \log N)$. Because problems in signal processing and time series analysis frequently process inputs of size $N = 1000$ or greater, the algorithm speeds up programs by factors of more than one hundred.

In Section 10.3.C of his *Numerical Methods, Software, and Analysis* (published in 1983 by McGraw-Hill), John Rice chronicles the algorithmic history of three-dimensional elliptic partial differential equations. Such problems arise in simulating VLSI devices, oil wells, nuclear reactors, and airfoils. A small part of that history (mostly but not entirely from his book) is given in the following table. The run time gives the number of floating point operations required to solve the problem on an $N \times N \times N$ grid.

METHOD	YEAR	RUN TIME
Gaussian Elimination	1945	N^7
SOR Iteration (Suboptimal Parameters)	1954	$8N^5$
SOR Iteration (Optimal Parameters)	1960	$8N^4 \log_2 N$
Cyclic Reduction	1970	$8N^3 \log_2 N$
Multigrid	1978	$60N^3$

SOR stands for "successive over-relaxation". The $O(N^3)$ time of Multigrid is within a constant factor of optimal because the problem has that many inputs. For typical problem sizes ($N=64$), the speedup is a factor of a quarter million. Pages 1090-1091 of "Programming Pearls" in the November 1984 *Communications of the ACM* present data to support Rice's argument that the algorithmic speedup from 1945 to 1970 exceeds the hardware speedup during that period.

Graph Algorithms. In a common method of building integrated circuitry, the designer describes an electrical circuit as a graph that is later transformed into a chip design. A popular approach to laying out the circuit uses the "graph partitioning" problem to divide the entire electrical circuit into subcomponents. Heuristic algorithms for graph partitioning developed in the early 1970's used $O(N^2)$ time to partition a circuit with a total of N components and wires. Fiduccia and Mattheyses describe "A linear-time heuristic for improving network partition" in the *19th Design Automation Conference*. Because typical problems involve a few thousand components, their method reduces layout time from a few hours to a few minutes.

Geometric Algorithms. Late in their design, integrated circuits are specified as geometric "artwork" that is eventually etched onto chips. Design systems process the artwork to perform tasks such as extracting the electrical circuit it describes, which is then compared to the circuit the designer specified. In the days when integrated circuits had $N=1000$ geometric figures that specified 100 transistors, algorithms that compared all pairs of geometric figures in $O(N^2)$ time could perform the task in a few minutes. Now that VLSI chips contain millions of geometric components, quadratic algorithms would take months. "Plane sweep" or "scan line" algorithms have reduced the run time to $O(N \log N)$, so the designs can now be processed in a few hours. Szymanski and Van Wyk's "Space efficient algorithms for VLSI artwork analysis" in the *20th Design Automation Conference* describes efficient algorithms for such tasks that use only $O(\sqrt{N})$ primary memory (a later version of the paper appears in the June 1985 *IEEE Design and Test*).

Appel's program described in Section 5.1 uses a tree data structure to represent points in 3-space and thereby reduces an $O(N^2)$ algorithm to $O(N \log N)$ time. That was the first step in reducing the run time of the complete program from a year to a day.

COLUMN 8: CODE TUNING

Some programmers pay too much attention to efficiency; by worrying too soon about little "optimizations" they create ruthlessly clever programs that are insidiously difficult to maintain. Others pay too little attention; they end up with beautifully structured programs that are utterly inefficient and therefore useless. Good programmers keep perspective on efficiency: it is just one of many problems in software, but it is sometimes very important.

Previous columns discuss high-level approaches to efficiency: problem definition, system structure, algorithm design, and data structure selection. This column is about a low-level approach. "Code tuning" locates the expensive parts of an existing program and then makes little changes to the code to improve its performance. It's not always the right approach to follow and it's rarely glamorous, but 't can sometimes make a big difference in a program's performance.

8.1 A Typical Story

Chris Van Wyk and I chatted about code tuning early one afternoon; he then wandered off to try it on a program. By 5:00 PM he had halved the run time of a three-thousand line program.

Given a textual description of a picture, his program produces commands to draw the picture on a phototypesetter. Although the run time for typical pictures was much shorter, the program took ten minutes to draw an extremely complicated picture. Van Wyk's first step was to *profile* the program by setting a compiler switch that caused the system to report how much time was spent in each procedure (like the second output in Solution 10). Running the program on ten test pictures showed that it spent almost seventy percent of its time in the memory allocation subroutine.

His next step was to study the memory allocator. A few lines of accounting code showed that the program allocated the most popular kind of record 68,000 times, while the runner-up was allocated only 2,000 times. Given that you knew that the majority of the program's time was spent looking through storage for a single type of record, how would you modify it to make it faster?

81

Van Wyk solved his problem by applying the principle of *caching*: data that is accessed most often should be the cheapest to access. He modified his program by caching free records of the most common type in a linked list. He could then handle the common request by a quick reference to that list rather than by invoking the general storage allocator; this reduced the total run time of his program to just 45 percent of what it had been previously (so the storage allocator now took just 30 percent of the total time). An additional benefit was that the reduced fragmentation of the modified allocator made more efficient use of main memory than the original allocator.

This story illustrates the art of code tuning at its best. By spending a few hours adding about twenty lines to a 3000-line program, Van Wyk doubled its speed without altering the users' view of the program or decreasing the ease of maintenance. He used general tools to achieve the speedup: profiling identified the "hot spot" of his program and caching reduced the time spent there.

8.2 A First Aid Quiz

We'll turn now from a beginning-to-end story to a quiz made of three composite stories. Each describes a typical problem that arises in several applications. The problems consumed most of the run time in their applications, and the solutions use general principles.

The first problem arises in text processing, compilers, macro processors, and command interpreters.

> *Problem One — Character Classification.* Given a sequence of one million characters, classify each as an upper-case letter, lower-case letter, digit, or other.

The obvious solution uses a complicated sequence of comparisons for each character. In the ASCII character code this approach uses six comparisons to determine that a particular character is of type "other", while the same result requires fourteen comparisons for EBCDIC. Can you do better?

One approach uses binary search — think about it. A faster solution views a character as an index into an array of character types; most programming languages provide a way to do this. For an example, let's assume that the character code has eight bits, so each character can be viewed as an integer in the range 0..255. *TypeTable*[0..255] is initialized with code in the spirit of the following fragment (although the wise programmer would try to do the job with loops).

```
for I := 0 to 255 do TypeTable[I] := Other
TypeTable['a'] := ... := TypeTable['z'] := LCLetter
TypeTable['A'] := ... := TypeTable['Z'] := UCLetter
TypeTable['0'] := ... := TypeTable['9'] := Digit
```

The type of the character C can then be found in *TypeTable*[C], which replaces a complicated sequence of character comparisons with a single array access.

This data structure typically reduces the time required to classify a character by an order of magnitude.

The next problem arises in applications ranging from set representation to coding theory.

> *Problem Two — Counting Bits.* Given a sequence of one million 32-bit words, tell how many one bits are in each word.

The obvious program uses a loop to do thirty-two shifts and logical ANDs; can you think of a better way?

The principle is the same as before: a table whose I^{th} entry contains the number of one bits in the binary representation of I. Unfortunately, most computers don't have enough room to store a table with 2^{32} entries, and the time to initialize the four billion entries would also be prohibitive. We can get around this by trading a few additional operations for a smaller table. We'll set up a table giving the counts for all eight-bit bytes, and then answer the 32-bit question by summing the answers to four eight-bit questions. The count table is initialized with two loops that have the effect of the following assignment statements; see Problem 2.

```
CountTable[0]    := 0;    CountTable[1]    := 1
CountTable[2]    := 1;    CountTable[3]    := 2
    . . .
CountTable[254]  := 7;    CountTable[255]  := 8
```

We could use a four-iteration loop to count the bits in all bytes of word W, but it is just as easy and probably a little faster to unroll the loop into

```
WordCount :=   CountTable[ W                and 11111111B]
             + CountTable[(W rshift  8) and 11111111B]
             + CountTable[(W rshift 16) and 11111111B]
             + CountTable[(W rshift 24) and 11111111B]
```

The code isolates the bytes by shifting and then ANDing off all but the eight low-order bits; this operation is language- and machine-dependent. While the original solution would use over a hundred machine instructions, the above approach can usually be implemented in about a dozen instructions; it is not uncommon for this change to result (again) in a speedup of an order of magnitude. (Several other approaches to counting bits are discussed by Reingold, Nievergelt and Deo in Section 1.1 of *Combinatorial Algorithms: Theory and Practice*, published in 1977 by Prentice-Hall.)

The final problem is typical of applications that deal with geographic or geometric data.

> *Problem Three — Computing Spherical Distances.* The first part of the input is a set S of five thousand points on the surface of a globe; each point is represented by its latitude and longitude. After those points are stored in a data structure of our choice, the program reads the second

part of the input: a sequence of twenty thousand points, each represented by latitude and longitude. For every point in that sequence, the program must tell which point in S is closest to it, where distance is measured as the angle between the rays from the center of the globe to the two points.

Margaret Wright of Stanford University encountered a problem similar to this in the preparation of maps to summarize data on the global distribution of certain genetic traits. Her straightforward solution represented the set S by an array of latitude and longitude values. The nearest neighbor to each point in the sequence was found by calculating its distance to every point in S using a complicated trigonometric formula involving ten sine and cosine functions. While the program was simple to code and produced fine maps for small data sets, it required several hours of mainframe time to produce large maps, which was well beyond the budget.

Because I had previously worked on geometric problems, Wright asked me to try my hand on this one. After spending much of a weekend on it, I developed several fancy algorithms and data structures for solving it. Fortunately (in retrospect), each would have required many hundreds of lines of code, so I didn't try to code any of them. When I described the data structures to Andrew Appel of Carnegie-Mellon University, he had a key insight: rather than approaching the problem at the level of data structures, why not use the simple data structure of keeping the points in an array, but tune the code to reduce the cost of computing the distance between points? How would you exploit this idea?

The cost can be greatly reduced by changing the representation of points: rather than using latitudes and longitudes, we'll represent a point's location on the surface of the globe by its x, y and z coordinates. Thus the data structure is an array that holds each point's latitude and longitude (which may be needed for other operations) as well as its three Cartesian coordinates. As each point in the sequence is processed, a few trigonometric functions translate its latitude and longitude into x, y and z coordinates, and we then compute its distance to every point in S. Its distance to a point in S is computed as the sum of the squares of the differences in the three dimensions, which is usually cheaper than computing one trigonometric function, let alone ten. This method computes the correct answer because the angle between two points increases monotonically with the square of their Euclidean distance.

Although this approach does require additional storage, it yields substantial benefits: when Wright incorporated the change into her program, the run time for complicated maps was reduced from several hours to half a minute. In this case, code tuning solved the problem with a couple of dozen lines of code, while algorithmic and data structure changes would have required many hundreds of lines.

8.3 Major Surgery — Binary Search

We'll turn from first aid to major surgery on a program that is one of the most subtle examples I know of code tuning. The details are from Problem 4.8: we are to perform a binary search in a table of one thousand integers. As we go through this exercise, keep in mind that this step is usually not needed in this program — the binary search algorithm is so efficient that code tuning is often superfluous. In Column 4, we therefore ignored microscopic efficiency and concentrated on achieving a simple, correct and maintainable program. Sometimes, though, the tuned version can make a big difference in a system.

We'll develop the fast binary search in a sequence of four programs. They are subtle, but there is good reason to follow them closely: the final program is usually two or three times faster than the binary search of Section 4.2. Before reading on, can you spot any obvious waste in that code?

```
L := 1; U := N
loop
    /* Invariant: if T is in X, it is in X[L..U] */
    if L > U then
        P := 0; break
    M := (L+U) div 2
    case
        X[M] < T:   L := M+1
        X[M] = T:   P := M; break
        X[M] > T:   U := M-1
```

Our development of the fast binary search will start with the modified problem of locating the *first* occurrence of the integer T in the integer array $X[1..N]$; the above code might return any one of multiple occurrences of T. The main loop of the program is similar to the one above; we'll keep indices L and U into the array that bracket the position of T, but we'll use the invariant relation that $X[L]<T$, $X[U]\geq T$ and $L<U$. We'll assume that $X[0]<T$ and that $X[N+1]\geq T$, but the program will never access those elements. The code is

```
L := 0; U := N+1
while L+1 ≠ U do
    /* Invariant: X[L] < T and X[U] >= T and L < U */
    M := (L+U) div 2
    if X[M] < T then
        L := M
    else
        U := M
/* assert L+1 = U and X[L] < T and X[U] >= T */
P := U
if P > N or X[P] ≠ T then P := 0
```

The first statement initializes the invariant. As the loop is repeated, the invariant is maintained by the if statement; it's easy to check that both branches maintain the invariant. Upon termination we know that if T is anywhere in the array, then its first occurrence is in position U; that fact is stated more formally in the `assert` comment. The final two statements set P to the index of the first occurrence of T in X if it is present, and to zero if it is not present. (The final statement must use a "conditional `or`" that does not evaluate the second clause if the first clause is true; see Problem 10.2.)

While this binary search solves a more difficult problem than the previous program, it is potentially more efficient: it makes only one comparison of T to an element of X in each iteration of the loop. The previous program sometimes had to test two such outcomes.

The next version of the program uses a different representation of a range: instead of representing $L..U$ by its lower and upper values, we'll represent it by its lower value L and an increment I such that $L+I=U$. The code will ensure that I is at all times a power of two; this property is easy to keep once we have it, but it is hard to get originally (because the array is of size $N=1000$). The program is therefore preceded by an assignment and `if` statement to ensure that the range being searched is initially of size 512, the largest power of two less than 1000; thus L and $L+I$ are either $0..512$ or $489..1001$. Translating the previous program to this new representation of a range yields this code.

```
I := 512
if X[512] >= T then
    L := 0
  else
    L := 1000+1-512
while I ≠ 1 do
    /* Invariant: X[L] < T and X[L+I] >= T and I = 2**j */
    NextI := I div 2
    if X[L+NextI] < T then
        L := L + NextI; I := NextI
      else
        I := NextI
/* assert I = 1 and X[L] < T and X[L+I] >= T */
P := L+1
if P > 1000 or X[P] ≠ T then P := 0
```

The correctness proof of this program has exactly the same flow as the proof of the previous program. This code is usually slower than its predecessor, but it opens the door for future speedups.

The next program is a simplification of the above, incorporating some optimizations that a smart compiler might perform. The first `if` statement is simplified, the variable *NextI* is removed, and the assignments to *NextI* are removed from the inner `if` statement.

```
I := 512; L := 0
if X[512] < T then L := 1000+1-512
while I ≠ 1 do
    /* Invariant: X[L] < T and X[L+I] >= T and I = 2**j */
    I := I div 2
    if X[L+I] < T then
        L := L+I
/* assert I = 1 and X[L] < T and X[L+I] >= T */
P := L+1
if P > 1000 or X[P] ≠ T then P := 0
```

Although the correctness argument for the code still has the same structure, we can now understand its operation on a more intuitive level. When the first test fails and *L* stays zero, the program computes the bits of *P* in left-to-right order, most significant bit first.

The final version of the code is not for the faint of heart. It removes the overhead of loop control and the division of *I* by two by unrolling the entire loop. In other words, because *I* assumes only a few distinct values in this particular problem, we can write them all down in the program, and thereby avoid computing them over and over again at run time.

```
L := 0
if X[512]   < T then L := 1000+1-512
    /* assert X[L] < T and X[L+512] >= T */
if X[L+256] < T then L := L+256
    /* assert X[L] < T and X[L+256] >= T */
if X[L+128] < T then L := L+128
if X[L+64]  < T then L := L+64
if X[L+32]  < T then L := L+32
if X[L+16]  < T then L := L+16
if X[L+8]   < T then L := L+8
if X[L+4]   < T then L := L+4
if X[L+2]   < T then L := L+2
    /* assert X[L] < T and X[L+2]   >= T */
if X[L+1]   < T then L := L+1
    /* assert X[L] < T and X[L+1]   >= T */
P := L+1
if P > 1000 or X[P] ≠ T then P := 0
```

We can understand this code by inserting the complete string of assertions like those surrounding the test of $X[L+256]$. Once you do the two-case analysis to see how that if statement behaves, all the other if statements fall into line.

I've compared the binary search of Section 4.2 with this fine-tuned binary search on several systems, with the following results.

MACHINE	LANGUAGE	OPTIMI- ZATIONS	UNITS	SLOW CODE	FAST CODE	SPEEDUP FACTOR
MIX	Assembly	Extreme	Tyme	18.0	4.0	4.5
TRS-80	BASIC	None	millisecs	43.6	14.6	3.0
PDP-10 (KL)	Pascal	None	microsecs	16.4	5.5	3.0
	Assembly	Extreme		4.5	0.9	5.0
VAX-11/750	C	None	microsecs	33.8	13.3	2.5
		Source code		22.5	12.2	1.8
		Compiler		29.2	12.8	2.3
		Both		19.7	12.2	1.6

The first line says that Knuth's assembly language implementation of the code in Section 4.2 runs in roughly $18.0 \log_2 N$ MIX Tyme units, while his implementation of the fast program in this section is 4.5 times faster. The speedup factor is dependent on many variables, but it is significant in all the above cases.

This derivation is an idealized account of code tuning at its most extreme. We replaced the obvious binary search program (which doesn't appear to have much fat on it) with a super-lean version that is several times faster.† The program verification tools of Column 4 played a crucial role in the task. Because we used them, we can believe that the final program is correct; when I first saw the final code presented without verification, I looked upon it as magic for months.

8.4 Principles

The most important principle about code tuning is that it should be done rarely. That sweeping generalization is explained by the following.

The Role of Efficiency. Many other properties of software are as important as efficiency, if not more so. Don Knuth has observed that premature optimization is the root of much programming evil; it can compromise the correctness, functionality and maintainability of programs. Save concern for efficiency for when it matters.

Profiling. When efficiency is important, the first step is to profile the system to find out where it spends its time. The solution to Problem 10 shows the output of two profilers. Such output usually shows that most of the time is going to a few hot spots and that the rest of the code is almost never executed (in Section 5.1, for instance, one procedure accounted for 98

---

† This program has been known in the computing underground since the early 1960's. Some of its history is sketched on page 93 of "Programming Pearls" in the February 1984 *Communications of the ACM*.

percent of the run time; in Section 6.4, 10 percent of the code accounted for 90 percent of the run time). Profiling points to the critical areas; for the other parts we follow the wise maxim of, "If it ain't broke, don't fix it."

Design Levels. We saw in Column 5 that there are many ways to solve efficiency problems. Before tuning code, we should make sure that other approaches don't provide a more effective solution.

The above discussion considers whether and when to tune code; once we decide to do so, that still leaves the question of how. I tried to answer that question in my book *Writing Efficient Programs* with a list of general rules for code tuning. All the examples we've seen can be explained in terms of those principles; I'll do that now with the names of the rules in *italics*.

Van Wyk's Drawing Program. The general strategy of Van Wyk's solution was to *Exploit Common Cases*; his particular exploitation involved *Caching* a list of the most common kind of record.

Problem One — Character Classification. The solution with a table indexed by a character *Precomputes A Logical Function*.

Problem Two — Counting Bits. The table of byte counts is closely related to the previous solution; it *Stores Precomputed Results*.

Problem Three — Computing Spherical Distances. Storing Cartesian coordinates along with latitudes and longitudes is an example of *Data Structure Augmentation*; using the cheaper Euclidean distance rather than the angular distance *Exploits An Algebraic Identity*.

Binary Search. *Combining Tests* reduced the number of array comparisons per inner loop from two to one, *Exploiting An Algebraic Identity* changed representations from a lower and upper bound to a lower bound and an increment, and *Loop Unrolling* expanded the program to remove all loop overhead.

So far we've tuned code to reduce CPU time. One can tune code for other purposes, such as reducing paging or increasing a cache hit ratio. Perhaps the most common use of code tuning beyond reducing run time is to reduce the space required by a program. Problem 4 gives a taste of that endeavor, and the next column is devoted to the topic.

8.5 Problems

1. The character classification program in the text assumed that the character classes were disjoint. How would you write a routine to test membership in overlapping character classes, such as lower case letters, upper case letters, letters, digits and alphanumerics?

2. Write a code fragment that given N, a power of two, initializes *CountTable*$[0..N-1]$ as described in the text.

3. How do the various binary search algorithms behave if they are (against specification) applied to unsorted arrays?

4. In the early days of programming, Fred Brooks faced the problem of representing a large table on a small computer. He couldn't store the entire table in an array because there was room for only a few bits for each table entry (actually, there was one decimal digit available for each entry — I said that it was in the early days!). His second approach was to use numerical analysis to fit a function through the table. That resulted in a function that was quite close to the true table (no entry was more than a couple of units off the true entry) and required an unnoticeably small amount of memory, but legal constraints meant that the approximation wasn't good enough. How could Brooks get the required accuracy in the limited space?

5. The typical sequential search to determine whether T is in $X[1..N]$ was given in Problem 4.9.

```
I := 1
while I <= N and X[I] ≠ T do I := I+1
```

A common example of code tuning speeds that up by placing T in a "sentinel" position at the end of the array.

```
X[N+1] := T
I := 1
while X[I] ≠ T do I := I+1
```

Eliminating the test $I <= N$ typically reduces the run time of the program by twenty or thirty percent. Implement the two programs and time them on your system.

6. How can sentinels be used in a program to find the maximum element in an array (see Problem 4.9)? How can sentinels decrease the search time in sets represented by linked lists, hash tables, and binary search trees?

7. Because sequential search is simpler than binary search, it is usually more efficient for small tables. On the other hand, the logarithmic number of comparisons made by binary search implies that it will be faster than the linear time of sequential search for large tables. The break-even point is a function of how much each program is tuned. How low and how high can you make that break-even point? What is it on your machine when both programs are equally tuned? Is it a function of the level of tuning?

8. D. B. Lomet of IBM Watson Research Center observes that hashing may solve the 1000-integer search problem more efficiently than the tuned binary search. Implement a fast hashing program and compare it to the tuned binary search; how do they compare in terms of speed and space?

9. In the early 1960's, Vic Berecz of the United Technologies Corporation found that most of the time in a simulation program at Sikorsky Aircraft was devoted to computing trigonometric functions. Further investigation

showed that the functions were computed only at integral multiples of five degrees. How did he reduce the run time?

10. Use a profiler to gather statistics on the performance of a program.

11. One sometimes tunes programs by thinking about mathematics rather than code. To evaluate the polynomial

$$y = a_n x^n + a_{n-1} x^{n-1} + \cdots + a_1 x^1 + a_0$$

the following code uses $2N$ multiplications. Give a faster routine.

```
Y := A[0]; XToTheI := 1
for I := 1 to N do
    XToTheI := X*XToTheI
    Y := Y + A[I]*XToTheI
```

12. Apply the techniques of this column to real programs. Try, for instance, the sorting program in Section 1.4 and the anagram program in Section 2.8.

8.6 Further Reading

Although I am willing to admit to a certain personal bias, my favorite book on code tuning is my own *Writing Efficient Programs*, published by Prentice-Hall in 1982. The heart of the book is a fifty-page discussion of the efficiency rules mentioned above; each is stated in general terms and then illustrated by application to small code fragments and by "war stories" of its application in real systems. Other parts of the book discuss the role of efficiency in software systems and the application of the rules to several important subroutines.

8.7 Tuning the Federal Government's COBOL Code *[Sidebar]*

The role of code tuning in data processing is discussed in the General Accounting Office report "Improving COBOL Applications Can Recover Significant Computer Resources" (1 April 1982, Order Code PB82-198540, National Technical Information Service, Springfield, Virginia 22161). These application systems are from the Department of Housing and Urban Development.

CPU TIME REDUCTION (Percent)	DOLLAR SAVINGS PER YEAR	COST TO OPTIMIZE
82	$37,400	$5,500
45	45,000	1,200
30	4,400	2,400
19	9,000	900
9	7,000	9,000

The optimizations cost a total of $19,000; over the four-year minimum life of the systems, they will save almost $400,000. In an Army application, one staff-day of optimization reduced the typical elapsed time of a program from 7.5 hours to less than two hours; this change saved $3,500 in its first year and resulted in the output being delivered to the user more reliably.

The report warns that code should not be tuned haphazardly; other considerations such as correctness and maintainability must be given their rightfully high priority. It points out that there is usually a point of diminishing returns in tuning either an individual program or a set of programs on a system: work beyond that point will be very difficult and have little positive impact.

The recommendations in the report include the following: "Heads of Federal agencies should require periodic review of the machine resource consumption of COBOL applications at their installations, and, where feasible, require action to reduce the consumption of the expensive applications."

COLUMN 9: **SQUEEZING SPACE**

If you're like several people I know, your first thought on reading the title of this column is "How old-fashioned!" In the bad old days of computing, so the story goes, programmers were constrained by small machines, but those days are long gone. The new philosophy is "a megabyte here, a megabyte there, pretty soon you're talking about real memory". And there is truth in that view — many programmers use big machines and rarely have to worry about squeezing space from their programs.

But every now and then, thinking hard about compact programs can be profitable. Sometimes the thought gives new insight that makes the program simpler.† Reducing space often has desirable side-effects on run time: smaller programs are faster to load, and less data to manipulate usually means less time to manipulate it. Even with cheap memories, space can be a critical. Many microprocessors have 64-kilobyte address spaces, and sloppy use of virtual memory on a large machine can lead to disastrously slow thrashing.

Keeping perspective on its importance, let's survey some techniques for reducing space.

9.1 The Key — Simplicity

Simplicity can yield functionality, robustness, speed and space. Fred Brooks observed this when he wrote a payroll program for a national company in the mid 1950's. The bottleneck of the program was the representation of the Kentucky state income tax. The tax was specified in the law by the obvious two-dimensional table (income as one dimension, number of exemptions as the other). Storing the table explicitly required thousands of words of memory, more than the capacity of the machine.

---

† In their paper about the UNIX operating system, which was developed on a small machine, Ritchie and Thompson remark that "there have always been fairly severe size constraints on the system and its software. Given the partially antagonistic desires for reasonable efficiency and expressive power, the size constraint has encouraged not only economy but a certain elegance of design." See page 374 of the July 1974 *Communications of the ACM.*

The first approach Brooks tried was to fit a mathematical function through the tax table, but it was so jagged that no simple function would come close. Knowing that it was made by legislators with no predisposition to crazy mathematical functions, Brooks consulted the minutes of the Kentucky legislature to see what arguments had led to the bizarre table. He found that the Kentucky tax was a simple function of the income that remained *after* federal tax was deducted. His program therefore calculated federal tax from existing tables, and then used the remaining income and a table of just a few dozen words of memory to find the Kentucky tax.

By studying the context in which the problem arose, Brooks was able to replace the original problem to be solved with a simpler problem. While the original problem appeared to require thousands of words of data space, the modified problem was solved with a negligible amount of memory.

Simplicity can also reduce code space. Column 3 describes several large programs that were replaced by small programs with more appropriate data structures. In those cases, a simpler view of the program reduced the source code from thousands to hundreds of lines and probably also shrank the size of the object code by an order of magnitude.

9.2 Data Space

Although simplification is usually the easiest way to solve a problem, some hard problems just won't yield to it. In this section we'll study techniques that reduce the space required to store the data accessed by a program; in the next section we'll consider reducing the memory space used to store the program as it is executing.

Don't Store, Recompute. The space required to store a given object can be dramatically reduced if we don't store it but rather recompute it whenever it is needed. In the early days of computing, some programs stored large tables of, for instance, the *sine* function. Today, virtually all programs compute trigonometric functions by calling a subroutine. This greatly reduces space requirements, and because of advances in numerical analysis and floating point hardware design, it is only slightly more expensive than interpolating from a large table. Similarly, a table of the prime numbers might be replaced by a subroutine for testing primality. This method trades more run time for less space, and it is applicable only if the objects to be "stored" can be recomputed from their description.

Such "generator programs" are often used in executing several programs on identical random inputs, for such purposes as performance comparisons or regression tests of correctness. Depending on the application, the random object might be a file of randomly generated lines of text or a graph with randomly generated edges. Rather than storing the entire object, we store just its generator program and the random seed that defines the particular object. By taking a little more time to access them, objects that have many megabytes can be represented in a few bytes.

Sparse Data Structures. Replacing a data structure can drastically reduce the space required to store given information. I once encountered a system that allowed the user to access any of two thousand points on a map by touching an input pad. The program converted the physical location selected to a pair of integers with x in the range 1..200 and y in the range 1..150 — the board was roughly four feet by three feet and the program used quarter-inch resolution. It then used that (x,y) pair to tell which, if any, of the two thousand points the user had chosen. Because no two points could be in the same (x,y) location, the programmer represented the map by a 200×150 array of point identifiers (an integer in the range 1..2000, or zero if no point was at that location). The bottom left corner of that array might look like this, where zero point identifiers are represented by empty squares.

In the corresponding map, point 17 is in location $(1,3)$, point 538 is in $(1,6)$, and the four other visible locations in the first column are empty.

Although the array was easy to implement and gave rapid access time, its $200 \times 150 = 30,000$ 16-bit words consumed over ten percent of the memory on the half-megabyte machine. When the system started to run out of space, the programmer hoped that we could reduce the storage in this structure. What would you suggest?

I'll describe our solution in FORTRAN terms because that was the language we used; if you use a language with more powerful data structuring facilities, take a minute to think about how you would express this solution. Here are the three arrays in our solution, with the integer indices in the bottom array also depicted as arrows.

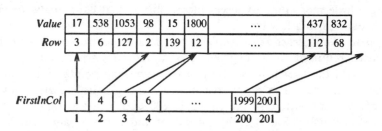

The points in column *I* are represented in the *Row* and *Value* arrays between locations *FirstInCol*[*I*] and *FirstInCol*[*I*+1]−1; even though there are only 200 columns, *FirstInCol*[201] is defined to make this condition hold. In the above picture there are three points in the first column: point 17 is in (1,3), point 538 is in (1,6), and point 1053 is in (1,127). There are two points in column 2, none in column 3, and two in column 200. To determine what point is stored in position (*I*,*J*) we use the following pseudocode.

```
for K := FirstInCol[I] to FirstInCol[I+1]-1 do
    if Row[K] = J then
        /* Found it in position K */
        return Value[K]
/* Unsuccessful search; (I,J) empty */
return 0
```

This method uses much less space than its predecessor: two 2000-element arrays and one 201-element array give 4201 16-bit words instead of 30,000. Although it is a little slower than its predecessor (in the very worst case an access costs 150 comparisons, but it uses half a dozen on the average), the program had no trouble keeping up with the user. Because of the good module structure of the system, this approach was incorporated in a few hours by changing a few subroutines. We observed no degradation in run time and gained fifty sorely needed kilobytes.

This solution illustrates several general points about data structures. The problem is classic: sparse array representation (a sparse array is one in which most entries have the same value, usually zero). The solution is conceptually simple and easy to implement using only arrays. Note that there is no *LastInCol* array to go with *FirstInCol*; we instead use the fact that the last point in this column is one before the first point in the next column. This is a trivial example of recomputing rather than storing. Similarly, there is no *Col* array to go with *Row*; because we only access *Row* through the *FirstInCol* array, we always know the current column.

Many other data structure techniques can reduce space. In Section 3.1 we saved space by storing a "ragged" three-dimensional table in a two-dimensional array. If we use a key to be stored as an index into a table, then we need not store the key itself; rather, we store only its relevant attributes, such as a count of how many times it has been seen. Applications of this *key indexing* technique were discussed in Sections 1.4 and 8.2 and Problems 1.7 and 1.8. **In** the sparse matrix example above, key indexing through the *FirstInCol* array allowed us to do without a *Col* array. Storing pointers to shared large objects (such as long text strings) removes the cost of storing many copies of the same object, although one has to be careful when modifying a shared object that all its owners desire the modification. This technique is used in my desk almanac to provide calendars for the years 1821 through 2080; rather than listing 260 distinct calendars it gives fourteen canonical calendars (seven days of the week for January 1 times leap year or non-leap year) and then a table giving a calendar number for each of the 260 years.

Data Compression. Insights from information theory reduce space by encoding objects compactly. In the sparse matrix example, for instance, we assumed that elements of *Row* were 16-bit integers. Because each row value is an integer in the range 1..150, that array could instead be represented by 8-bit bytes, which would save another kilobyte. In a microcomputer-based business system I encoded the two decimal digits A and B in one byte (instead of the obvious two) by the integer $N = 10 \times A + B$. The information was decoded by the two statements

```
A := N div 10
B := N mod 10
```

This simple scheme squeezed a file of numeric data onto one floppy disk instead of two.† Such encodings can reduce the space required by individual records, but the small records usually take more time to process because they must first be decoded.

Information theory can also compress a stream of records being transmitted over a channel such as a telecommunications line or a disk file. Such compression techniques are typically subtle to implement, but they can lead to substantial savings: Column 13 sketches how a file of 30,000 English words was squeezed into 26,000 16-bit computer words. Details on these techniques can be found in the references.

Allocation Policies. Sometimes how much space you use isn't as important as how you use it. Suppose, for instance, that your program uses three different types of records, X, Y, and Z, all of the same size. In some languages your first impulse might be to declare, say, one hundred objects of each of the three types. But what if you used 101 X's and no Y's or Z's? The program could run out of space after using 101 records, even though 200 others were completely unused. *Dynamic allocation* of records avoids such obvious waste by allocating records as they are needed. Most modern languages provide such

---

† Several readers suggested using the encoding $N = (A \text{ lshift } 4)$ or B; the values can be decoded by the statements $A := N \text{ rshift } 4$ and $B := N \text{ and } 1111_2$. John Linderman observes that "not only are shifting and masking commonly faster than multiplying and dividing, but common utilities like a hex dump could display the encoded data in a readable form".

a mechanism, but even in primitive languages such as FORTRAN, a programmer can implement such a policy in a user-level routine.

Dynamic allocation says that we shouldn't ask for something until we need it; the policy of *variable-length records* says that when we do ask for something, we should ask for only as much as we need. In the days of eighty-column records it was common for more than half the bytes on a program library disk to be trailing blanks. Variable-length files denote the end of lines by a "new line" character and thereby double the storage capacity of such disks. I once tripled the speed of a microcomputer program by using tape records of variable length: the maximum record length was 250, but only about 80 bytes were used on the average.

More advanced allocation techniques are described in the references. *Garbage collection* recycles discarded storage so that the old bits are as good as new. The Heapsort algorithm in Section 12.4 *overlays* two logical data structures used at separate times in the same physical storage locations. For another approach to *sharing* storage, Brian Kernighan once wrote a traveling salesman program in which the lion's share of the space was devoted to two $N \times N$ matrices, where N was 150. The two matrices, which I'll call A and B to protect their anonymity, represented distances between points. Kernighan therefore knew that they had zero diagonals ($A[I,I]=0$) and that they were symmetric ($A[I,J]=A[J,I]$). He therefore let the two triangular matrices share space in one square matrix, C, one corner of which looked like

0	B[1,2]	B[1,3]	B[1,4]	
A[2,1]	0	B[2,3]	B[2,4]	
A[3,1]	A[3,2]	0	B[3,4]	
A[4,1]	A[4,2]	A[4,3]	0	

Kernighan could then refer to $A[I,J]$ by the code

```
C[max(I,J), min(I,J)]
```

and similarly for B, but with the *min* and *max* swapped. This representation has been used in various programs since the dawn of time. The technique made Kernighan's program somewhat more difficult to write and slightly slower, but the reduction from two 22,500-word matrices to just one was significant on a 30,000-word machine. And if the matrices were 900×900, the same change would have the same effect today on a four-megabyte machine.

9.3 Code Space

Sometimes the space bottleneck of a program is not its data but rather the size of the program itself. For instance, I subscribe to hobbyist magazines that publish graphics programs with page after page of code like

```
for I := 17 to 43 do Set(I,68)
for I := 18 to 42 do Set(I,69)
for J := 81 to 91 do Set(30,J)
for J := 82 to 92 do Set(31,J)
```

where $Set(X,Y)$ turns on the picture element at screen position (X,Y). Appropriate subroutines, say Hor and $Vert$ for drawing horizontal and vertical lines, would allow that code to be replaced by

```
Hor(17,43,68)
Hor(18,42,69)
Vert(81,91,30)
Vert(82,92,31)
```

This code could in turn be replaced by an interpreter that read commands from a text file like

```
H  17 43 68
H  18 42 69
V  81 91 30
V  82 92 31
```

If that still took too much space, each of the lines could be represented in a 32-bit word by allocating two bits for the command (H, V, or two others) and ten bits for each of the three numbers, which are integers in the range 0..1023. (The translation would, of course, be done by a program.) This hypothetical case illustrates several general techniques for reducing code space.

Subroutine Definition. Replacing a common pattern in the code by a subroutine simplified the above program and thereby reduced its space and increased its clarity. This is a trivial instance of "bottom-up" design. Although one can't ignore the many merits of "top-down" methods, the homogeneous world view given by good primitive routines can make a system easier to maintain and simultaneously reduce space.

Featurecide reduces code space by removing functionality from subroutines. Sections 9.6 and 9.7 give references on this delicate topic.

Interpreters. In the hypothetical case above we were able to replace a long line of program text with a four-byte command to a special-purpose interpreter. Section 3.2 describes an interpreter for producing form letters; although its main purpose is to make a program simpler to build and to maintain, it incidentally reduces the program's space.

Translation to Machine Language. One aspect of space reduction over which most programmers have relatively little control is the translation from the source language into the machine language. For instance, some minor compiler changes reduced the code space of early versions of the UNIX system by as much as five percent. As a last resort, a programmer might consider coding a large system into assembly language by hand, but this is an expensive, error-prone process that usually yields only small dividends. In an unpublished experiment, Lynn Robert Carter (then of Motorola Software Technology) found that spending ten weeks recoding 1500 lines of Pascal into 2900 lines of assembly code reduced the size of the object module from 16,000 to 12,000 bytes. Those four kilobytes were crucial in the application (the system had run a few kilobytes over the 128K on the processor board and there was no room in the chassis for a memory board), but the effort works out to ten bytes per hour, or roughly five dollars per byte.

9.4 Principles

Now that we've seen the techniques for reducing space, let's consider the attitude we should have as we approach the problem.

The Cost of Space. What happens if a program uses ten percent more space? On many systems such an increase will have no cost: previously wasted bits are now put to good use. On small systems the program might not work at all: it runs out of memory. On large time-sharing systems the cost might rise by exactly ten percent. On virtual-memory systems the run time might increase dramatically because the program that previously fit in physical memory now makes many disk accesses — Problem 2.4 describes how increasing the problem size of a program by a few percent increased its run time by two orders of magnitude. Know the cost of space before you set out to reduce it.

The ''Hot Spots'' of Space. Section 8.4 described how the run time of programs is usually clustered in hot spots: a few percent of the code accounts for much of the run time. The opposite is true in the space required by code: whether an instruction is executed a billion times or not at all, it requires the same space to store. Data space can have hot spots: a few common records may account for most of the storage. In the sparse matrix example, for instance, a single data structure accounted for more than ten percent of the storage used on a half-megabyte machine. Replacing it with a structure one-tenth the size had a substantial impact on the system; reducing a one-kilobyte structure by a factor of a hundred would have had negligible impact.

Tradeoffs. Sometimes a programmer must trade away performance, functionality or maintainability to gain space; such engineering decisions should be made only after all alternatives are studied. Several examples in this column showed how reducing space can sometimes have a positive impact on the other dimensions. In Section 1.4, a bitmap data structure allowed a set of records to be stored in internal memory rather than on disk and thereby reduced the run time from minutes to seconds and the code from hundreds to dozens of lines. This happened only because the original solution was far from optimal, but we programmers who are not yet perfect often find our code in exactly that state. We should acknowledge that fact and look for techniques that improve all aspects of our solutions before we trade away any desirable properties.

Work with the Environment. The programming environment can have a substantial impact on the space efficiency of a program. Important issues include the representations used by a compiler and run-time system, memory allocation policies, and paging policies. When you're almost out of space, make sure that you know enough about these issues to ensure that you aren't working against the system.

Use the Right Tool for the Job. We've seen four techniques that reduce data space (Recomputing, Sparse Structures, Information Theory, and Allocation Policies), three techniques that reduce code space (Subroutine Definition, Interpreters, and Translation) and one overriding principle (Simplicity). When space is critical, consider all your options.

9.5 Problems

1. In the late 1970's Stu Feldman built a FORTRAN 77 compiler that barely fit in a 64-kilobyte code space. To reduce space he had packed the elements of several kinds of records into four-bit fields. When he unpacked the records by storing the fields in eight-bit bytes, he found that although the data space had increased by a few hundred bytes, the overall size of the program went down by several thousand bytes. What happened?

2. Questions about the sparse matrix example: Are there other simple but space-efficient data structures for the task? How would you write a program to build the data structure described in the text? How would you change the structure so that it could be searched more quickly without using too much additional storage? Suppose storage became even more scarce — how much further can you reduce the space?

3. Study data in non-computer applications such as almanacs or mathematical tables for examples of squeezing space.

4. A BASIC program in a hobbyist magazine contained DATA statements that together define a sequence of about four thousand one-byte integers. The first few integers in the sequence are

    128, 128, 128, 128, 128, 128, 128, 128, 128, 128, 128, 128, 128, 128, 128, 128,
    128, 128, 128, 128, 128, 128, 128, 128, 128, 128, 128, 128, 128, 128, 128, 128,
    128, 128, 128, 128, 128, 128, 152, 166, 172, 153, 164, 128, 128, 128, 128, 128,
    128, 128, 128, 128, 128, 128, 128, 128, 128, 128, 128, 128, 128, 128, 128, ...

    The program listed the numbers in four pages of double-column text. What are more appropriate representations?

5. The discussion of "Data Compression" in Section 9.2 mentioned decoding $10 \times A + B$ with a *div* and a *mod* operation. Discuss the time and space tradeoffs involved in replacing those operations by table lookups.

6. Design a linked list that has only one "pointer" per node yet can be traversed in forward or reverse order.

7. In a common type of program *profiler*, the value of the instruction counter is sampled on a regular basis; see, for instance, Solution 8.10. Design a data structure for storing those values that is efficient in time and space and also provides useful output.

8. The (remarkably handsome) face in Section 3.3 is stored in 48×48 bytes. Suppose that you had to store many faces with similar characteristics; how far could you reduce the space requirements?

9. COBOL programmers typically allocate six bytes for a date in the twentieth century (MMDDYY), nine bytes for a social security number (DDD-DD-DDDD), and 21 bytes for a name (12 for last, 8 for first, and 1 for middle initial). If space is critical, how far can you reduce those requirements?

10. [A. Appel] Compress an online dictionary of English to be as small as possible. When counting space, measure both the data file and the program that interprets the data.

9.6 Further Reading

Many data structures texts discuss techniques for reducing data space. Standish's *Data Structures Techniques* (published in 1980 by Addison-Wesley) is particularly strong in this area. Relevant sections include 2.5 (managing several stacks), 5.4 (storage reclamation), 5.5 (compacting and coexistence), 6.2 (dynamic storage allocation), 7.2 (string representation), 7.4 (variable-length string representation), and 8.3 through 8.5 (array representation).

Chapter 9 of Fred Brooks's *Mythical Man Month* (published by Addison-Wesley in 1975) is entitled "Ten pounds in a five-pound sack"; it concentrates on managerial control of space in large projects. He raises such important issues as size budgets, module function specification, and trading space for function or time.

9.7 Two Big Squeezes [Sidebar]

The body of this column surveys various techniques; let's now inspect two space-critical systems to see how the techniques come into play.

Ken Thompson has developed a two-phase program that solves chess endgames† for given configurations such as a King and two Bishops matched against a King and a Knight. The learning phase of the program computes the distance to checkmate for all possible chessboards (over the given set of four or five pieces) by working backwards from all possible checkmates; computer scientists will recognize this technique as dynamic programming, while chess

---

† This program is distinct from the Belle chess machine developed by Joe Condon and Thompson.

experts know it as retrograde analysis. The resulting database makes the program omniscient with respect to the given pieces, so in the game-playing phase it plays perfect endgames. The game it plays is described by chess experts with terms like "complex, fluid, lengthy and difficult" and "excruciating slowness and mystery", and it has already upset established chess dogma.

Explicitly storing all possible chessboards was prohibitively expensive in space. Thompson therefore used an encoding of the chessboard as a key to index a disk file of board information; each record in the file contained 12 bits, including the distance to checkmate from that position. Because there are 64 squares on a chessboard, the positions of five fixed pieces can be encoded by five integers in the range 0..63 that give the location of each piece. The resulting key of 30 bits implies a table of 2^{30} or about 1.07 billion 12-bit records in the database, which exceeded the capacity of the disk.

Thompson's key insight was that chessboards that are mirror images around any of the dotted lines in the following figure have the same value and need not be duplicated in the database.

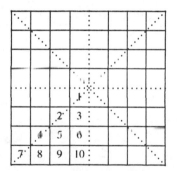

His program therefore assumed that the white King was in one of the ten numbered squares; an arbitrary chessboard can be put into this form by a sequence of at most three reflections. This normalization reduces the disk file to 10×64^4 or 10×2^{24} 12-bit records. Thompson further observed that because the black King cannot be adjacent to the white King, there are only 454 legal board positions for the two Kings in which the white King is in one of the ten squares marked above. Exploiting that fact, his database shrunk to 454×64^3 or about 121 million 12-bit records, which fit comfortably on a single (dedicated) disk.

For a second space-critical system, we'll consider Apple's Macintosh computer; details on the machine and its design history can be found in the February 1984 issue of *BYTE*. The space constraint in that system was the fact that an enormous amount of system functionality had to be squeezed into a 64 kilobyte Read-Only Memory (ROM). The design team achieved this by careful subroutine definition (involving generalizing operators, merging routines and featurecide) and hand coding the entire ROM in assembly language. They estimate that their extremely tuned code, with careful register allocation and choice of instructions, is half the size of equivalent code compiled from a high-level language.

These two systems differ in many ways. The Mac design team was motivated to squeeze 128 kilobytes of code into a 64K ROM because they anticipated shipping millions of copies. Even though Thompson knew there would be just one copy of his program, he had to squeeze a file onto one disk. The Mac team tuned assembly code to reduce ROM space; Thompson exploited symmetry in data structures to reduce disk space.

The two efforts do share some attributes, though. Both cases reduced space by a small constant factor (2 for the Mac ROM, 8 for the endgame disk) that was critical for the success of the entire system. Squeezing space also reduced the run time of both systems. The tight assembly code in the Mac can perform input/output at a megabit per second, and decreasing the number of positions in the endgame program reduced the time of its learning phase from a year to a few weeks.

PART III: **THE PRODUCT**

Now comes the fun. Parts I and II laid a foundation; the next four columns use that material to build interesting programs. The problems are important, and they provide focal points where the techniques of previous columns converge in real applications.

Columns 10, 11 and 12 describe general-purpose subroutines for sorting, searching, and priority queues. Column 13 is the history of a program for checking spelling; it uses several of those set algorithms in various forms. Columns 11 and 13 are built around particular applications, while Columns 10 and 12 are driven by the methods underlying their programs.

Column 10 appeared in the April 1984 *Communications of the ACM*, Column 11 in December 1984, Column 12 in March 1985, and Column 13 in May 1985.

How should you sort a sequence of records into order? The answer is usually straightforward:

Use a sort command provided by the system.

Unfortunately, this plan doesn't always work. Some systems don't have a sort command, and existing sorts may not be general enough or efficient enough to solve a particular problem (as in Section 1.1). In such cases, a programmer has no choice but to write a sort routine.

10.1 Insertion Sort — An $O(N^2)$ Algorithm

Insertion Sort is the method most card players use to sort their cards. They keep the cards dealt so far in sorted order, and as each new card arrives they insert it into its proper relative position. To sort the array $X[1..N]$ into increasing order we'll start with the sorted subarray $X[1..1]$ and then insert the elements $X[2]$, ..., $X[N]$, as in the following pseudocode.

```
for I := 2 to N do
    /* Invariant: X[1..I-1] is sorted */
    /* Goal: sift X[I] down to its
            proper place in X[1..I-1] */
```

The following four lines show the progress of the algorithm on a four-element array. The "*" represents the variable I; elements to its left are sorted, while elements to its right are in their original order.

```
3*1 4 2
1 3*4 2
1 3 4*2
1 2 3 4*
```

The sifting down is accomplished by a right-to-left loop that uses the variable J to keep track of the element being sifted. The loop swaps the element with its predecessor in the array as long as there is a predecessor (that is, $J>1$) and the element hasn't reached its final position (that is, it is out of order with its predecessor). Thus the entire sort is

107

```
for I := 2 to N do
    /* Invariant: X[1..I-1] is sorted */
    J := I
    while J > 1 and X[J-1] > X[J] do
        Swap(X[J], X[J-1])
        J := J-1
```

When I need to sort and efficiency isn't an issue, that's the routine I use; it's just five lines of easy code. (In a few zealously protective languages this code may generate a run-time error; see Problem 2.)

If you don't have a *Swap* routine handy, the following assignments use the variable T to exchange $X[J]$ and $X[J-1]$.

```
T := X[J];   X[J] := X[J-1];   X[J-1] := T
```

This code opens the door for a simple exercise in the code tuning of Column 8. Because the variable T is assigned the same value over and over (the value originally in $X[I]$), we can move the assignments to and from T out of the loop, and change the comparison as follows.

```
for I := 2 to N do
    /* Invariant: X[1..I-1] is sorted */
    J := I
    T := X[J]
    while J > 1 and X[J-1] > T do
        X[J] := X[J-1]
        J := J-1
    X[J] := T
```

This code shifts elements right into the hole vacated by $X[I]$, and finally moves T into the hole once it is in its final position. It is seven lines long and a little more subtle than the simple Insertion Sort, but on my system it takes just one third the time of the first program.

This routine is easy to translate, even into primitive languages such as this dialect of BASIC.

```
1000 ' SORT X(1..N), N>1
1010 FOR I=2 TO N
1015    ' INVARIANT: X(1..I-1) IS SORTED
1020    J=I
1030    T=X(J)
1040    IF J<=1 OR X(J-1)<=T THEN 1080
1050       X(J)=X(J-1)
1060       J=J-1
1070       GOTO 1040
1080    X(J)=T
1090 NEXT I
1100 RETURN
```

When I compared the run time of this program with an "efficient" sort from a 1982 BASIC text (whose sneaky logic used twice as many lines of code), I found that this simple routine required less than half the run time of its more complex cousin.

On random data as well as in the worst case, the time of Insertion Sort on an N-element array is proportional to N^2. Fortunately, if the array is already almost sorted, the program is much faster because each element sifts down just a short distance

10.2 Quicksort — An $O(N \log N)$ Algorithm

This algorithm was described by C. A. R. Hoare in his classic paper "Quicksort" in the *Computer Journal 5*, 1, April 1962, pp. 10-15. It uses the *divide-and-conquer* schema of Section 7.3: to sort an array we divide it into two smaller pieces and sort those recursively. For instance, to sort the eight-element array

we *partition* it around the first element (55) so that all elements less than 55 are to the left of it, while all greater elements are to its right

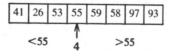

If we then recursively sort the subarray from 1 to 3 and the subarray from 5 to 8, independently, the entire array is sorted.

The average run time of this algorithm is much less than the $O(N^2)$ time of Insertion Sort because a partitioning operation goes a long way towards sorting the sequence. After a typical partitioning of N elements, there are about $N/2$ elements above the partition value and $N/2$ elements below it. In a similar amount of run time, the sift operation of Insertion Sort manages to get just one more element into the right place.

The above idea leads to a sketch of a recursive subroutine. We'll represent the portion of the array we're dealing with by the two indices L and U, for the lower and upper limits. The recursion stops when we come to an array with fewer than two elements. So the code is

```
procedure QSort(L,U)
    if L >= U then
        /* at most one element, do nothing */
    else
        /* partition array around a given
           value, which is eventually
           placed in its correct position P
        */
        QSort(L, P-1)
        QSort(P+1, U)
```

To partition the array around the value T we'll use a simple scheme that I learned from Nico Lomuto of Alsys, Inc. There are faster programs for this job[†], but this routine is so easy to understand that it's hard to get wrong, and it is by no means slow. Given the value T, we are to rearrange $X[A..B]$ and compute the index M (for "middle") such that all elements less than T are to one side of M, while all other elements are on the other side. We'll accomplish the job with a simple for loop that scans the array from left to right, using the variables I and M to maintain the following invariant in array X.

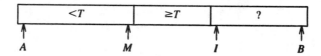

When the code inspects the Ith element there are two cases to consider. If $X[I] \geq T$ then all is fine; the invariant is still true. On the other hand, when $X[I] < T$, we can regain the invariant by incrementing M to index the new location of the small element, and then swapping that element with $X[I]$. The complete partitioning code is

```
M := A-1
for I := A to B do
    if X[I] < T then
        M := M+1
        Swap(X[M], X[I])
```

---

† Most presentations of Quicksort use a partitioning scheme based on two approaching indices, like the one described in Problem 3. Although the basic idea of that scheme is simple, I have always found the details tricky — I once spent the better part of two days chasing down a bug hiding in a short partitioning loop. A reader of a preliminary draft complained that the standard two-index method is in fact simpler than Lomuto's, and sketched some code to make his point; I stopped looking after I found two bugs.

In Quicksort we'll partition the array $X[L..U]$ around the value $T=X[L]$, so A will be $L+1$ and B will be U. Thus the invariant of the partitioning loop is depicted as

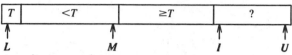

When the loop terminates we have

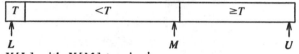

We then swap $X[L]$ with $X[M]$ to give†

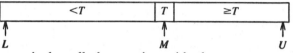

We can now recursively call the routine with the parameters $(L,M-1)$ and $(M+1,U)$.

The above algorithm always partitions around the first element in the array. This choice can require excessive time and space for some common inputs — for instance, arrays that are already sorted. We do far better to choose a partitioning element at random; we accomplish this by swapping $X[L]$ with a random entry in $X[L..U]$. If you don't have the *RandInt* function used in the code below, you can make one using a function *Rand* that returns a random real distributed uniformly in $[0,1)$ by the expression $L+int(Rand\times(U+1-L))$. In the unlikely event that your system doesn't even have that routine, consult Knuth's *Seminumerical Algorithms*. But whether you use a system routine or make your own, be careful that *RandInt* returns a value in the range $L..U$ — a value out of range is an insidious bug.

The final code, Quicksort 1, is presented on the next page. To sort the array $X[1..N]$ we call the procedure

```
QSort(1,N)
```

---

† It is tempting to ignore this step and to recur with parameters (L,M) and $(M+1,U)$; this gives an infinite loop when T is the strictly greatest element in the subarray. I would have caught the bug had I tried to verify termination, but the astute reader can guess how I really discovered it. Miriam Jacob found an elegant proof of incorrectness: since $X[L]$ is never moved, the sort can only work if the minimum element in the array starts in $X[1]$.

```
procedure QSort(L,U)
    if L < U then
        Swap(X[L], X[RandInt(L,U)])
        T := X[L]
        M := L
        for I := L+1 to U do
            /* Invariant: X[L+1..M] < T and
                          X[M+1..I-1] >= T */
            if X[I] < T then
                M := M+1
                Swap(X[M], X[I])
        Swap(X[L], X[M])
        /* X[L..M-1] < X[M] <= X[M+1..U] */
        QSort(L, M-1)
        QSort(M+1, U)
```

Most of the proof of correctness of this program was given in its derivation (which is, of course, its proper place). The proof proceeds by induction: the outer if statement correctly handles empty and single-element arrays, and the partitioning code correctly sets up larger arrays for the recursive calls. The program can't make an infinite sequence of recursive calls because the element $X[M]$ is excluded at each invocation; this is the same argument that Section 4.3 used to show that binary search terminates.

Let's turn now to the performance of the program. I won't give the details here, but Quicksort runs in $O(N \log N)$ time and $O(\log N)$ stack space on the average, for any input array with distinct elements. The mathematical arguments are similar to those in Section 7.3, and Solution 10 contains data on one implementation. The random performance is a result of calling the random number generator, rather than an assumption about the distribution of inputs. Problems 3, 5 and 11 show ways of improving Quicksort's worst-case performance. Most algorithms texts analyze Quicksort's run time mathematically, and also prove the lower bound that any comparison-based sort must use $O(N \log N)$ comparisons; Quicksort is therefore close to optimal.

Fans of Column 8 have probably noticed several ways to tune the Quicksort code to make it faster. The simplest is indicated in Solution 8.10: we should expand the code for the *Swap* procedure in the inner loop (because the other two calls to *Swap* aren't in the inner loop, writing them in line would have a negligible impact on the speed). On my system this reduced the run time to two-thirds of what it was previously. We might also observe that a great deal of time is spent sorting very small subarrays. It would be faster to sort those using a simple method like Insertion Sort rather than firing up all the machinery of Quicksort.

Bob Sedgewick developed a particularly clever implementation of this idea. When Quicksort is called on a small subarray (that is, when U and L are near), we do nothing. We implement this by changing the first if statement in the Quicksort procedure to

```
if U-L > CutOff then
```

where *CutOff* is a small integer. When the program finishes the array will not be sorted, but it will be grouped into small clumps of randomly ordered values such that the elements in one clump are less than elements in any clump to its right. We must clean up within the clumps by another sort method; because the array is almost sorted, Insertion Sort is just right for the job. We sort the entire array by the code

```
QSort(1,N)
InsertionSort
```

To determine the best choice for *CutOff*, I ran the program twice at all values of *CutOff* from 1 to 50, with *N* fixed at 5000. This graph plots the results.

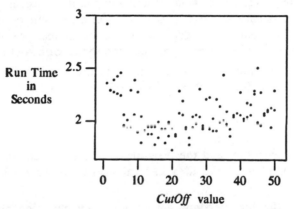

A good value of *CutOff* was 15; values between 10 and 20 give savings to within a few percent of that. This change reduced the program, which we'll call Quicksort 2, to half of its original time, or another twenty-five percent reduction after writing the *Swap* procedure in line.

10.3 Principles

The programs we've studied are summarized in the following table. They were implemented in C on a VAX-11/750 and timed on random 32-bit integers; the logarithms are base two. Insertion Sort 1 is the first sort given; Insertion Sort 2 writes the *Swap* code in line and moves assignments to and from *T* out of the loop. Quicksort 1 is the first Quicksort; Quicksort 2 writes the *Swap* code in line and sorts small subarrays by calling Insertion Sort 2 after the recursive call on (1,*N*). The System Sort is the UNIX system's *qsort*. The run-time functions are the result of fitting the known form of the functions to the observed times in the table.

PROGRAM	LINES OF C CODE	RUN TIME IN MICROSECONDS	TIME IN SECONDS FOR SIZE		
			100	1000	10000
Insertion Sort 1	5	$17N^2$	0.17	17.3	1730
Insertion Sort 2	7	$6N^2$	0.06	5.7	570
Quicksort 1	11	$63N \log_2 N$	0.05	0.63	7.8
Quicksort 2	20	$32N \log_2 N$	0.03	0.32	4.3
System Sort	1	$97N \log_2 N$	0.06	1.0	13.6

We'll see yet another $O(N \log N)$ sort in Section 12.4.

There are several important lessons to be learned from the table, about both sorting in particular and programming in general.

The system sort is easy and relatively fast; it is slower than the hand-made Quicksorts only because its general and flexible interface uses a procedure call for each comparison. If a system sort can meet your needs, don't even consider writing your own code. (Section 2.8 describes two sorts available on the UNIX system: the `sort` program and the `qsort` routine.)

Insertion Sort is simple to code and may be fast enough for small sorting jobs. Sorting 10,000 integers with Insertion Sort 2 requires just ten minutes on my system.

For large N, the $O(N \log N)$ run time of Quicksort is crucial. The algorithm design techniques of Column 7 gave us the basic idea for this divide-and-conquer algorithm, and the program verification techniques of Column 4 helped us implement the idea in straightforward, succinct and efficient code.

Even though the big speedups are achieved by changing algorithms, the code tuning techniques of Column 8 speed up Insertion Sort by a factor of 3 and Quicksort by a factor of 2.

10.4 Problems

1. Like any other powerful tool, sorting is often used when it shouldn't be and often not used when it should be. Explain how sorting could be either overused or underused when calculating the following statistics of an array of N floating point numbers: minimum, maximum, mean, median and mode.

2. Suppose that $X[1..10]$ and T are declared to be integers; what happens when the following code is executed?

```
I := 11
if I <= 10 and X[I] < T then I := I+1
```

In many languages the code will execute gracefully without altering I. On some systems, though, the code might abort because the array index I is out of bounds. What would yours do? Why is this an issue in the various Insertion Sorts? How can the problem be fixed in those sorts?

3. The Quicksort program in the text runs in time proportional to N^2 if $X[1]=X[2]=...=X[N]$; explain why. That problem is avoided in Problem 11 and in the following Quicksort, which is adapted from Sedgewick's paper cited in Section 10.5.

```
procedure QSort(L, U)
    if L < U then
        Swap(X[L], X[RandInt(L,U)])
        I := L; J := U+1; T := X[L]
        loop
            repeat I := I+1 until X[I] >= T
            repeat J := J-1 until X[J] <= T
            if J < I then break
            Swap(X[I], X[J])
        Swap(X[L], X[J])
        QSort(L, J-1)
        QSort(I, U)
```

This code assumes that no key in X is greater than $X[N+1]$; it uses that position as a sentinel element to increase the speed of the inner loop. On arrays of distinct elements, this code makes fewer swaps than Quicksort 1 and is therefore almost twice as fast. Use the techniques of Column 4 to prove that this program is correct. How does it solve the problem of duplicate keys?

4. [R. Sedgewick] Speed up Lomuto's partitioning scheme by using $X[L]$ as a sentinel like that described in Problem 8.5. Show how this scheme allows you to remove the *Swap* after the loop.

5. Although Quicksort uses only $O(\log N)$ stack space on the average, it can use linear space in the worst case. Explain why, then modify the program to use only logarithmic space in the worst case.

6. [M. D. McIlroy] Show how to use Lomuto's partitioning scheme to sort varying-length bit strings in time proportional to the sum of their lengths.

7. Implement several sorting programs and summarize them in a table like that in the text. In addition to Insertion Sort and Quicksort, you may want to consider Shell Sort (fair speed with simple code), Heapsort (minimal extra space and good worst-case speed — see Section 12.4), and Radix Sort (applicable only in special cases, but fast for those — see Solution 6). Does your table support the same conclusions?

8. Sketch a one-page procedure to show a user of your system how to select a sorting routine. Make sure that your method considers the importance of run time, space, programmer time (development and maintenance), generality (what if I want to sort character strings that represent Roman numerals?), stability (items with equal keys should retain their relative

order), special properties of the input data, etc. As an extreme test of your procedure, try feeding it the sorting problem described in Column 1.

9. Write a program for finding the Kth-smallest element in the array $X[1..N]$ in $O(N)$ expected time. Your algorithm may permute the elements of X. Present data on its run time.

10. Gather and display empirical data on the run time of a Quicksort program.

11. Write a "fat pivot" partitioning routine with the postcondition

$<T$	$=T$	$>T$

How would you incorporate the routine into a Quicksort program?

12. Study sorting methods used in non-computer applications (such as mail rooms and change sorters).

13. The Quicksort programs in this column choose a partitioning element at random. Study better choices, such as the median element of a sample from the array.

10.5 Further Reading

What to read about sorting depends on why you're reading. To learn more about the subject in general, see the algorithms texts cited in Columns 2 and 7. The following references are particularly helpful for programmers writing sort routines.

If you want to write the ultimate primary-memory sort routine, see Sedgewick's "Implementing Quicksort Programs" in the October 1978 *Communications of the ACM*.

If your job is to write a simple disk-based sort, see Chapter 4 of Kernighan and Plauger's *Software Tools* or *Software Tools in Pascal*.

Programmers who are about to spend several months writing a quality system sort should study Knuth's *Art of Computer Programming, volume 3: Sorting and Searching*. Linderman's "Theory and practice in the construction of a working sort routine" (in *The Bell Laboratories Technical Journal 63*, 8, part 2, pp. 1827-1843) tells about putting that material to work in a real system sort.

Small computer programs are often educational and entertaining. This column tells the story of a tiny program that, in addition to those qualities, proved quite useful to a small company.

11.1 The Problem

The company had just purchased several personal computers. After I got their primary system up and running, I encouraged people to keep an eye open for tasks around the office that could be done by a program. The firm's business was public opinion polling, and an alert employee suggested automating the task of drawing a random sample from a printed list of precincts. Because doing the job by hand required a boring hour with a table of random numbers, she proposed the following program.

> I'd like a program to which the user types a list of precinct names and an integer M. Its output is a list of M of the precincts chosen at random. There are usually a few hundred precinct names (each an alphanumeric string of at most a dozen characters), and M is typically between 20 and 40.

That's the user's idea for a program. Do you have any suggestions about the problem definition before we dive into coding?

My primary response was that it was a great idea; the task was ripe for automation. I then pointed out that typing several hundred names, while perhaps easier than dealing with long columns of random numbers, was still a tedious and error-prone task. In general, it's foolish to prepare a lot of input when the program is going to ignore the bulk of it anyway. I therefore suggested an alternative program.

> The input consists of two integers M and N, with $M<N$. The output is a sorted list of M random integers in the range $1..N$ in which no integer occurs more than once. For probability buffs, we desire a sorted selection without replacement in which each selection occurs equiprobably.

117

When $M=20$ and $N=200$, the program might produce a 20-element sequence that starts 4, 15, 17, ... The user then draws a sample of size 20 from 200 precincts by counting through the list and marking the 4th, 15th, and 17th names, and so on. (The output is required to be sorted because the hardcopy list isn't numbered.)

That specification met with the approval of its potential users. After the program was implemented, the task that previously required an hour could be accomplished in a few minutes.

Now look at the problem from the other side: how would you implement the program? Assume that your system provides a function $RandInt(I,J)$ that returns a random integer chosen uniformly in the range $I..J$, and a function $RandReal(A,B)$ that returns a random real number chosen uniformly in the interval $[A,B)$.

11.2 One Solution

As soon as we settled on the problem to be solved, I ran to my nearest copy of Knuth's *Seminumerical Algorithms* (having copies of Knuth's three volumes both at home and at work has been well worth the investment). Because I had studied the book carefully a decade earlier, I knew that it contained several algorithms for problems like this. After spending a minute considering several possible designs that we'll study shortly, I realized that Algorithm S in Knuth's Section 3.4.2 was the ideal solution to this problem.

The algorithm considers the integers 1, 2, ..., N in order, and selects each one by an appropriate random test. By visiting the integers in order, we guarantee that the output will be sorted.

To understand the selection criterion, let's consider the example that $M=2$ and $N=5$. We should select the integer 1 with probability 2/5; a program implements that by a statement like

```
if RandReal(0,1) < 2/5 then ...
```

Unfortunately, we can't select 2 with the same probability: doing so might or might not give us a total of 2 out of the 5 integers. We will therefore bias the decision and select 2 with probability 1/4 if 1 was chosen but with probability 2/4 if 1 was not chosen. In general, to select S numbers out of R remaining, we'll select the next number with probability S/R.

This probabilistic idea results in Program 1.

```
Select := M; Remaining := N
for I := 1 to N do
    if RandReal(0,1) < Select/Remaining then
        print I; Select := Select-1
    Remaining := Remaining-1
```

As long as $M \le N$, the program selects exactly M integers: it can't select more because when *Select* goes to zero no integer is selected and it can't select fewer because when *Select/Remaining* goes to one an integer is always selected. The `for` statement ensures that the integers are printed in sorted order. The above description should help you believe that each subset is equally likely to be picked; Knuth gives a probabilistic proof.

Knuth's second volume made the program easy to write. Even including titles, range checking and the like, the final program required only thirteen lines of BASIC. It was finished half an hour after the problem was defined, and has been used for several years without problems.

11.3 The Design Space

One part of a programmer's job is solving today's problem. Another, and perhaps more important, part of the job is to prepare for solving tomorrow's problems. Sometimes that preparation involves taking classes or studying books like Knuth's. More often, though, we programmers learn by the simple mental exercise of asking how we might have solved a problem differently. Let's do that now by exploring the space of possible designs for the sampling problem.

When I talked about the problem at West Point, I asked for a better approach than the first problem statement (typing all 200 names to the program). One student suggested photocopying the precinct list, cutting the copy with a paper slicer, shaking the slips in a paper bag, and then pulling out the required number of slips. That cadet showed the "conceptual blockbusting" that is the subject of Adams's book cited in Section 1.7.†

From now on we'll confine our search to a program to write *M* sorted integers at random from 1..*N*. We'll start by evaluating Program 1. The algorithmic idea is straightforward, the code is short, it uses just a few words of space, and the run time is fine for this application. The run time might, however, be a problem in other applications: to select a dozen integers from the range $1..2^{31}-1$, for instance, would take hours on a supercomputer. It's therefore worth a few minutes of our time to study other ways of solving the problem. Sketch as many high-level designs as you can before reading on; don't worry about implementation details yet.

One solution inserts random integers into an initially empty set until there are enough. In pseudocode, it is

---

† Page 57 of that book sketches Arthur Koestler's views on three kinds of creativity. *Ah!* insights are his name for originality, and *aha!* insights are acts of discovery. He would call this cadet's solution a *haha!* insight: the low-tech answer to a high-tech question is an act of comic inspiration (as in Solution 1.10).

```
Initialize set S to empty
Size := 0
while Size < M do
    T := RandInt(1,N)
    if T is not in S then
        Insert T in S
        Size := Size + 1
Print the elements of S in sorted order
```

The algorithm is not biased towards any particular element; its output is random. We are still left with the problem of implementing the set S; think about an appropriate data structure.

The bitmap data structure described in Section 1.4 is particularly easy to implement. We represent the set S by an array of bits in which the Ith bit is one if and only if the integer I is in the set. We initialize it by the subroutine *InitToEmpty*, which turns off all bits.

```
for I := 1 to N do
    Bit[I] := 0
```

The function *Member*(*T*) tells whether T is in S by returning $Bit[T]$, and the procedure *Insert*(*T*) inserts T in S by the assignment $Bit[T]:=1$. Finally, the routine *PrintInOrder* prints the elements of S.

```
for I := 1 to N do
    if Bit[I] = 1 then
        print I
```

These subroutines allow us to write more precise pseudocode for Program 2.

```
InitToEmpty
Size := 0
while Size < M do
    T := RandInt(1,N)
    if not Member(T) then
        Insert(T)
        Size := Size + 1
PrintInOrder
```

The bitmaps in Program 2 use N/b words of b-bit memory. The obvious implementations of the initialization and printing routines both require time proportional to N, but that can be reduced to N/b by simultaneously operating on all b bits in a word (this holds as long as $M < N/b$; we'll soon consider what to do when M is close to N). There are always exactly M calls to the *Insert* procedure, but there may be more calls to *Member* because some of *RandInt*'s random numbers may already be in the set. Problem 2 shows that as long as $M < N/2$, the expected number of *Member* tests is less than $2M$. Both *Member* and *Insert* require constant time per operation, so their total cost is proportional to M. Thus the expected total run time of Program 2 is $O(N/b)$.

Although the performance analysis assumed that the set was implemented by a bitmap, nothing in Program 2 says so. The *InitToEmpty*, *Member*, *Insert* and *PrintInOrder* operations all refer to an "abstract data type" of sets (a set with these operations is usually called a *dictionary*, more on this in Section 12.5). Replacing those four subroutines can change the representation of the sets and thereby change the performance of the program. This figure illustrates several possible data structures at the end of a run in which $M=5$, $N=10$, and *RandInt*(1,10) returns the sequence 3, 1, 4, 1, 5, 9.

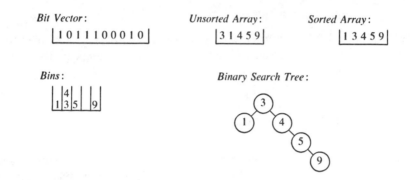

Binary search trees are described in most texts on algorithms and data structures. Because the insertions into the tree are in random order, it is unlikely to get too far out of balance; complex balancing schemes are therefore not needed in this application. The M bins can be viewed as a kind of hashing in which the integers in the range $1..N/M$ are placed in the first bin, and the integer I hashes to bin (roughly) $I \times M/N$. The bins are implemented as an array of linked lists. Because the integers are uniformly distributed, each linked list has expected length one. The average performance of the various schemes, when $M < N/b$, is as follows.

Set Representation	O(Time Per Operation)				Total Time	Space In Words
	Init	Member	Insert	Print		
Bit Vector	N/b	1	1	N/b	$O(N/b)$	N/b
Unsorted Array	1	M	1	$M \log M$	$O(M^2)$	M
Sorted Array	1	$\log M$	M	M	$O(M^2)$	M
Binary Tree	1	$\log M$	$\log M$	M	$O(M \log M)$	$3M$
Bins	M	1	1	M	$O(M)$	$3M$

Beware of the constant factors hiding in the big-ohs: the array operations are usually cheap compared to some implementations of the bit vector accesses, the pointer operations on binary trees, and the divisions used by bins. To understand the performance issues, let's consider the case that $N=1,000,000$ and $b=32$. When $M=5,000$, bins are probably the most efficient structure;

when $M = 50,000$, bitmaps are faster and take less space; when $M = 500,000$, Program 1 uses much less space and is also faster. When $M = 999,995$, though, we would do better to represent the five elements *not* selected; either kind of array would be easy to code and fast for this task.

Yet another approach to generating a sorted subset of random integers is to shuffle an N-element array that contains the numbers $1..N$, and then sort the first M to be the output. Knuth's Algorithm P in Section 3.4.2 shuffles the array $X[1..N]$.

```
for I := 1 to N do
    Swap(X[I], X[RandInt(I,N)])
```

Ashley Shepherd and Alex Woronow of the University of Houston observed that in this problem we need shuffle only the first M elements of the array, which gives Program 3.

```
for I := 1 to N do X[I] := I
for I := 1 to M do
    Swap(X[I], X[RandInt(I,N)])
Sort(1, M)
```

The sorted list is in $X[1..M]$. The algorithm uses N words of memory and $O(N + M \log M)$ time, but the technique of Problem 1.8 reduces this to $O(M \log M)$ time. We can view this algorithm as an alternative to Program 2 in which we represent the set of selected elements in $X[1..I]$ and the set of unselected elements in $X[I+1..N]$. By explicitly representing the unselected elements we avoid testing whether the new element was previously chosen.

Programs 1, 2 and 3 offer different solutions to the problem, but they by no means cover the possible design space. Yet another approach generates the "gaps" between successive integers in the set. J. S. Vitter's "Faster Methods for Random Sampling" in the July 1984 *Communications of the ACM* generate M sorted random integers in $O(M)$ time and constant space; those resource bounds are within a constant factor of optimal.

11.4 Principles

This column illustrates several important steps in the programming process. Although the following discussion presents the stages in one natural order, the design process is more active: we hop from one activity to another, usually iterating through each many times before arriving at an acceptable solution.

Understand the Perceived Problem. Talk with the user about the context in which the problem arises. Problem statements often include ideas about solutions; like all early ideas, they should be considered but not followed slavishly.

Specify an Abstract Problem. A clean, crisp problem statement helps us first to solve this problem and then to see how this solution can be applied to other problems.

Explore the Design Space. Too many programmers jump too quickly to "the" solution to their problem; they think for a minute and code for a day rather than thinking for an hour and coding for an hour. Using informal high-level languages helps us to describe designs succinctly: pseudocode represents control flow and "abstract data types" represent the crucial data structures. Knowledge of the literature is invaluable at this stage of the design process.

Implement One Solution. On lucky days our exploration of the design space shows that one program is far superior to the rest; at other times we have to prototype the top few to choose the best. We should strive to implement the chosen design in straightforward and succinct code.†

Retrospect. Polya's delightful *How To Solve It* can help any programmer become a better problem solver. On page 15 he observes that "There remains always something to do; with sufficient study and penetration, we could improve any solution, and, in any case, we can always improve our understanding of the solution." His hints are particularly helpful for looking back at programming problems.

11.5 Problems

1. Section 11.1 specified that all *M*-element subsets be chosen with equal probability, which is a stronger requirement than choosing each integer with probability *M/N*. Describe an algorithm that chooses each element equiprobably, but chooses some subsets with greater probability than others.

2. Show that when $M < N/2$, the expected number of *Member* tests made by Program 2 before finding a number not in the set is less than 2.

3. Counting the *Member* tests in Program 2 leads to many interesting problems in combinatorics and probability theory. How many *Member* tests does the program make on the average as a function of *M* and *N*? How many does it make when $M = N$? When is it likely to make more than *M* tests?

4. This column described several algorithms for one problem. Implement some, measure their performance, and describe when each is appropriate as a function of constraints on run time, space, coding time, etc.

---

† Problem 5 describes a class exercise that I graded on programming style. Most students turned in one-page solutions and received mediocre grades. Two students who had spent the previous summer on a large software development project turned in beautifully documented five-page programs, broken into a dozen procedures, each with an elaborate heading. They received failing grades. My program worked in five lines of code, and their inflation factor of sixty was too much for a passing grade. When they complained that they were employing standard software engineering tools, I should have quoted Pamela Zave: "The purpose of software engineering is to control complexity, not to create it." A few more minutes spent looking for a simple program might have spared them hours documenting their complex program.

5. [Class Exercise] I assigned the problem of generating sorted subsets twice in an undergraduate course on algorithms. Before the unit on sorting and searching, students had to write a program for $M=20$ and $N=400$; the primary grading criterion was a short, clean program — run time was not an issue. After the unit on sorting and searching they had to solve the problem again with $M=2000$ and $N=1,000,000$, and the grade was based primarily on run time.

6. [V. A. Vyssotsky] Algorithms for generating combinatorial objects are often profitably expressed as recursive procedures. Program 1 can be written as

```
procedure RandSelect(M, N)
        pre   0 <= M <= N
        post  M distinct integers from 1..N are
              printed in decreasing order
    if M > 0 then
        if RandReal(0,1) < M/N then
            print N; RandSelect(M-1, N-1)
        else
            RandSelect(M, N-1)
```

This program prints the random integers in decreasing order; how could you make them appear in increasing order? Argue the correctness of the resulting program. How could you use the basic recursive structure of this program to generate all M-element subsets of $1..N$?

7. How would you generate a random selection of M integers from $1..N$ with the constraint that the final output must appear in random order? How would you generate a sorted list if duplicate integers were allowed in the list? What if both duplicates and random order were desired?

8. [M. I. Shamos] A promotional game consists of a card containing ten spots, which hide a random permutation of the integers $1..10$. The player rubs the dots off the card to expose the hidden integers. If the integer 3 is ever exposed then the card loses; if 1 and 2 (in either order) are revealed then the card wins. Describe the steps you would take to compute the probability that randomly choosing a sequence of spots wins the game; assume that you may use at most one hour of CPU time.

11.6 Further Reading

Combinatorial Algorithms for Computers and Calculators by Nijenhuis and Wilf (Second Edition published by Academic Press in 1978) presents a large collection of algorithms both abstractly and as ready-to-run FORTRAN programs. It is particularly strong in algorithms for generating combinatorial objects, such as random selections.

COLUMN 12: **HEAPS**

This column is about "heaps", a data structure that we'll use to solve two problems.

Sorting. Heapsort sorts an N-element array in $O(N \log N)$ time and uses just a few words of extra space.

Priority Queues. Heaps maintain a set of elements under the operations of inserting new elements and extracting the smallest element in the set; each operation requires $O(\log N)$ time.

For both problems, heaps are simple to code and computationally efficient.

This column has a "bottom-up" organization: we'll start at the details and work up to the big picture. The next two sections describe the heap data structure and two routines to operate on it. The two subsequent sections use those tools to solve the problems mentioned above.

12.1 The Data Structure

A heap is a data structure for representing a collection of items.† Our examples will represent numbers, but the elements in a heap may be of any ordered type. Here's a heap of twelve integers

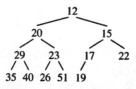

That binary tree is a heap by virtue of two properties. We'll call the first property *Order*: the value at any node is less than or equal to the values of the node's children. This implies that the least element of the set is at the root of

---

† In other computing contexts, the word "heap" refers to a large segment of memory from which variable-size nodes are allocated; we'll ignore that interpretation in this column.

the tree (12 in the example), but it doesn't say anything about the relative order of left and right children. The second heap property is *Shape*; the idea is captured by the picture

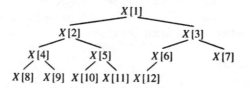

In words, a binary tree with the *Shape* property has its terminal nodes on at most two levels, with those on the bottom level as far left as possible. There are no "holes" in the tree; if it contains N nodes, no node is of distance more than $\log_2 N$ from the root. We'll soon see how the two properties together are restrictive enough to allow us to find the minimum element in a set, but lax enough so that we can efficiently reorganize the structure after inserting or deleting an element.

Let's turn now from the abstract properties of heaps to their implementation. There are, of course, many possible representations of binary trees, such as records and pointers. We'll use an implementation that is suitable only for binary trees with the *Shape* property, but is quite effective for that special case. A 12-element tree with *Shape* is implemented in the 12-element array X as

```
                          X[1]
              X[2]                    X[3]
         X[4]      X[5]        X[6]      X[7]
      X[8] X[9] X[10] X[11] X[12]
```

In this *implicit* representation of a binary tree, the root is in $X[1]$, its two children are in $X[2]$ and $X[3]$, and so on. Various functions on the tree are defined as follows.

```
Root = 1
Value(I) = X[I]
LeftChild(I) = 2*I
RightChild(I) = 2*I+1
Parent(I) = I div 2
Null(I) = (I<1) or (I>N)
```

An N-element implicit tree necessarily has the *Shape* property: there is no provision for missing elements.

This picture shows a 12-element heap and its implementation as an implicit tree in a 12-element array.

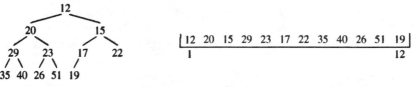

Because the *Shape* property is guaranteed by the representation, from now on we'll use the name *Heap* to mean that the value in any node is greater than or equal to the value in its parent. Phrased precisely, the array $X[1..N]$ has the *Heap* property if

$$\forall_{2 \leq i \leq N} \; X[i \text{ div } 2] \leq X[i]$$

In the next section we'll want to talk about $X[L..U]$ having the heap property (it doesn't have the shape property); we'll define $Heap(L,U)$ as

$$\forall_{2L \leq i \leq U} \; X[i \text{ div } 2] \leq X[i]$$

12.2 Two Critical Routines

In this section we'll study two routines for fixing an array whose *Heap* property has been broken at one end or the other. Both routines are efficient: they require roughly log N time to re-organize a heap of N elements. In the bottom-up spirit of this column, we'll define the routines here and then use them in the next sections.

Placing an arbitrary element in $X[N]$ when $X[1..N-1]$ is a heap will probably not yield $Heap(1,N)$; establishing the property is the job of procedure *SiftUp*. Its name describes its strategy: we sift the new element up the tree as far as it should go, swapping it with its parent along the way. (Take a second to contemplate which way is up: the root of the heap is at the top of the tree, and therefore $X[N]$ is at the bottom of the array.) The process is illustrated in the following pictures, which (left to right) show the new element 13 being sifted up the heap until it is at its proper position as the right child of the root.

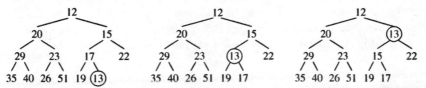

The process continues until the circled node is greater than or equal to its parent (as in this case) or it is at the root of the tree. If the process starts with $Heap(1,N-1)$ true, it leaves $Heap(1,N)$ true.

With that intuitive background, let's write the code. The sifting process calls for a loop, so we'll start with the loop invariant. In the picture above, the heap property holds everywhere in the tree except between the circled node and its parent. If we let *I* be the index of the circled node, then we can use the invariant

```
loop
     /* Invariant: Heap(1,N) except perhaps
          between I and its parent */
```

Because we originally have *Heap*(1,$N-1$), we initialize the loop by the assignment I:=N.

The loop must check whether we have finished yet (either by the circled node being at the top of the heap or greater than or equal to its parent) and, if not, make progress towards termination. The invariant says that the *Heap* property holds everywhere except perhaps between *I* and its parent. If the test $I=1$ is true, then *I* has no parent and the *Heap* property thus holds everywhere; the loop may therefore terminate. When *I* does have a parent, we'll let *P* be the parent's index by assigning P := I div 2. If $X[P]\leq X[I]$ then the heap property holds everywhere, and the loop may terminate.

If, on the other hand, *I* is out of order with its parent, then we swap $X[I]$ and $X[P]$. This step is illustrated in the following picture, in which the keys are single letters and node *I* is circled.

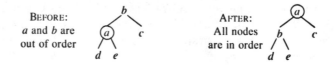

BEFORE:
a and *b* are
out of order

AFTER:
All nodes
are in order

After the swap, all five elements are in the proper order: $b<d$ and $b<e$ because *b* was originally higher in the heap†, $a<b$ because the test $X[P]\leq X[I]$ failed, and $a<c$ by combining $a<b$ and $b<c$. This gives the heap property everywhere in the array except possibly between *P* and its parent; we therefore regain the invariant by assigning I:=P.

The above pieces are assembled in this *SiftUp* code, which runs in time proportional to log *N* because the heap has that many levels.

---

† This important property is unstated in the loop invariant. Don Knuth observes that to be precise, the invariant should be strengthened to "*Heap*(1,*N*) holds if *I* has no parent; otherwise it would hold if $X[I]$ were replaced by $X[P]$, where *P* is the parent of *I*". Similar precision should also be used in the *SiftDown* loop we'll study shortly.

```
procedure SiftUp(N)
        pre    Heap(1,N-1) and N > 0
        post   Heap(1,N)
    I := N
    loop
        /* Invariant: Heap(1,N) except perhaps
                   between I and its parent */
        if I = 1 then break
        P := I div 2
        if X[P] <= X[I] then break
        Swap(X[P], X[I])
        I := P
```

As in Column 4, the "pre" and "post" lines characterize the procedure: if the precondition is true before the routine is called then the postcondition will be true afterwards.

Assigning a new value to $X[1]$ when $X[1..N]$ is a heap leaves $Heap(2,N)$; procedure *SiftDown* makes $Heap(1,N)$ true. It does so by sifting $X[1]$ down the array until either it has no children or it is less than or equal to the children it does have. The following pictures show 18 being sifted down the heap until it is finally less than its single child, 19.

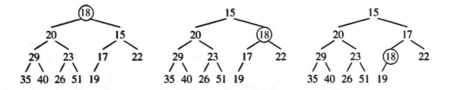

When an element is sifted up, it always goes towards the root. Sifting down is more complicated: an out-of-order element is swapped with its lesser child.

The pictures illustrate the invariant of the *SiftDown* loop: the heap property holds everywhere except, possibly, between the circled node and its children.

```
loop
    /* Invariant: Heap(1,N) except perhaps between
               I and its (0, 1 or 2) children */
```

The loop is similar to *SiftUp*'s. We first check whether I has any children, and terminate the loop if it has none. Now comes the subtle part: if I does have children, then we set the variable C to index the least child of I. Finally, we either terminate the loop if $X[I] \leq X[C]$, or progress towards the bottom by swapping $X[I]$ and $X[C]$ and assigning I:=C.

```
procedure SiftDown(N)
        pre   Heap(2,N) and N >= 0
        post  Heap(1,N)
    I := 1
    loop
        /* Invariant: Heap(1,N) except perhaps between
                 I and its (0, 1 or 2) children */
        C := 2*I
        if C > N then break
        /* C is the left child of I */
        if C+1 <= N then
            /* C+1 is the right child of I */
            if X[C+1] < X[C] then
                C := C+1
        /* C is the least child of I */
        if X[I] <= X[C] then break
        Swap(X[C], X[I])
        I := C
```

A case analysis like that done for *SiftUp* shows that the swap operation leaves the heap property true everywhere except possibly between *C* and its children. Like *SiftUp*, this procedure takes time proportional to log *N*, because it does a fixed amount of work at each level of the heap.

12.3 Priority Queues

There are two sides to any data structure. Looking from the outside, its *abstraction* tells what it does — a queue maintains a sequence of elements under the operations of insert and extract. On the inside, its *implementation* tells how it does it — a queue might use an array or a linked list. We'll start our study of priority queues by specifying their abstract properties, and then turn to implementations.

A priority queue manipulates an initially empty set† of elements, which we'll call *S*. The *Insert* procedure inserts a new element into the set; we can define that more precisely in terms of its pre- and postconditions.

```
procedure Insert(T)
        pre   |S| < MaxSize
        post  Current S = Original S ∪ {T}
```

Procedure *ExtractMin* deletes the smallest element in the set and returns that value in its single parameter *T*.

---

† Because the set can contain multiple copies of the same element, we would be more precise to call it a "multiset" or a "bag". The union operator is defined so that {2,3} ∪ {2} = {2,2,3}.

```
procedure ExtractMin(T)
        pre   |S| > 0
        post  Original S = Current S ∪ {T}
              and T = min(Original S)
```

This procedure could, of course, be modified to yield the maximum element, or any extreme element under a total ordering.

Priority queues are useful in many applications. An operating system may use such a structure to represent a set of tasks; they are inserted in an arbitrary order, and the task with highest priority is extracted to be executed. In discrete event simulation, the elements are times of events: the simulation loop extracts the event with the least time and possibly adds more events to the queue. In both applications the basic priority queue must be augmented to contain additional information beyond the elements in the set; we'll ignore that "implementation detail" in our discussion.

Sequential structures such as arrays or linked lists are obvious candidates for implementing priority queues. If the sequence is sorted it is easy to extract the minimum but hard to insert a new element; the situation is reversed for unsorted structures. This table shows the performance of the structures on an N-element set.

DATA STRUCTURE	RUN TIMES		
	1 Insert	1 ExtractMin	N of Each
Sorted Sequence	$O(N)$	$O(1)$	$O(N^2)$
Heaps	$O(\log N)$	$O(\log N)$	$O(N \log N)$
Unsorted Sequence	$O(1)$	$O(N)$	$O(N^2)$

Even though binary search can find the position of an inserted element in a sorted array in $O(\log N)$ time, moving the old elements to make way for the new may require $O(N)$ steps. If you've forgotten the difference between $O(N^2)$ and $O(N \log N)$ algorithms, review Section 7.5: for $N = 100,000$, the run times of those programs are 1.5 days and 1.3 minutes.

The heap implementation of priority queues provides a middle ground between the two sequential extremes. It represents an N-element set in the array $X[1..N]$ with the heap property, where X is declared as $X[1..MaxSize]$. We initialize the set to be empty by the assignment N:=0. To insert a new element we increment N and place the new element in $X[N]$. That gives the situation that *SiftUp* was designed to fix: $Heap(1, N-1)$. The insertion code is therefore

```
procedure Insert(T)
    if N >= MaxSize then error
    N := N+1; X[N] := T
    /* Heap(1,N-1) */
    SiftUp(N)
    /* Heap(1,N) */
```

Procedure *ExtractMin* finds the minimum element in the set, deletes it, and restructures the array to have the heap property. Because the array is a heap, the minimum element is in $X[1]$. The $N-1$ elements remaining in the set are now in $X[2..N]$, which has the heap property. We regain $Heap(1,N)$ in two steps. We first move $X[N]$ to $X[1]$ and decrement N; the elements of the set are now in $X[1..N]$, and $Heap(2,N)$ is true. The second step calls *SiftDown*. The code is straightforward.

```
procedure ExtractMin(T)
    if N < 1 then error
    T := X[1]
    X[1] := X[N]; N := N-1
    /* Heap(2,N) */
    SiftDown(N)
    /* Heap(1,N) */
```

Both *Insert* and *ExtractMin* require $O(\log N)$ time when applied to heaps that contain N elements.

12.4 A Sorting Algorithm

Priority queues provide a simple algorithm for sorting $A[1..N]$.

```
for I := 1 to N do
    Insert(A[I])
for I := 1 to N do
    ExtractMin(A[I])
```

The N *Insert* and *ExtractMin* operations have a worst-case cost of $O(N \log N)$, which is superior to the $O(N^2)$ worst-case time of the Quicksort in Section 10.2. Unfortunately, the array $X[1..N]$ used for heaps requires N additional words of storage.

In this section we'll study the Heapsort algorithm, which can be viewed as an improvement of the above approach: it uses less code, it uses less space because it doesn't require the auxiliary array, and it uses less time — see Problem 2. For purposes of this algorithm we'll assume that *SiftUp* and *SiftDown* have been modified to operate on heaps in which the *largest* element is at the top; that is easy to accomplish by swapping "<" and ">" signs.

The simple algorithm uses two arrays, one for the priority queue and one for the elements to be sorted. Heapsort saves space by using just one. The single implementation array X represents two abstract structures: a heap at the left end and at the right end the sequence of elements, originally in arbitrary order and finally sorted. This picture shows the evolution of the array X; the array is drawn horizontally, while time marches down the vertical axis.

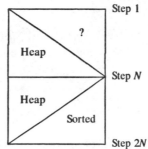

The Heapsort algorithm is a two-stage process: the first N steps build the array into a heap, and the next N steps extract the elements in decreasing order and build the final sorted sequence, right to left.

The first stage builds the heap. Its invariant can be drawn as

This code establishes $Heap(1,N)$.

```
for I := 2 to N do
    /* Invariant: Heap(1,I-1) */
    SiftUp(I)
    /* Heap(1,I) */
```

The second stage uses the heap to build the sorted sequence. Its invariant can be drawn as

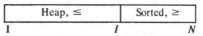

The loop body maintains the invariant in two operations. Because $X[1]$ is the largest among the first I elements, swapping it with $X[I]$ extends the sorted sequence by one element. That swap compromises the heap property, which we regain by sifting down the new top element. The code for the second stage is

```
for I := N downto 2 do
    /* Heap(1,I)  , Sorted(I+1,N) and X[1..I]<=X[I+1..N] */
    Swap(X[1], X[I])
    /* Heap(2,I-1), Sorted(I,N)   and X[1..I-1]<=X[I..N] */
    SiftDown(I-1)
    /* Heap(1,I-1), Sorted(I,N)   and X[1..I-1]<=X[I..N] */
```

The complete Heapsort algorithm requires just five lines of code.

```
for I := 2 to N do
    SiftUp(I)
for I := N downto 2 do
    Swap(X[1], X[I])
    SiftDown(I-1)
```

Because the algorithm uses $N - 1$ *SiftUp* and *SiftDown* operations, each of cost at most $O(\log N)$, it runs in $O(N \log N)$ time, even in the worst case.

12.5 Principles

Efficiency. The *Shape* property guarantees that all nodes in a heap are within $\log_2 N$ levels of the root; procedures *SiftUp* and *SiftDown* have efficient run times precisely because the trees are balanced. Heapsort avoids using extra space by overlaying two abstract structures (a heap and a sequence) in one implementation array.

Correctness. To write code for a loop we first state its invariant precisely; the loop then makes progress towards termination while preserving its invariant. The *Shape* and *Order* properties represent a different kind of invariant: they are invariant properties of the heap data structure. A routine that operates on a heap may assume that the properties are true when it starts to work on the structure, and it must in turn make sure that they remain true when it finishes.

Abstraction. Good engineers distinguish between *what* a component does (the abstraction seen by the user) and *how* it does it (the implementation inside the black box). In this column we've seen two ways to package black boxes: procedural abstraction and abstract data types.

Procedural Abstraction. We can use a sort procedure to sort an array without knowing its implementation: we view the sort as a single operation. Procedures *SiftUp* and *SiftDown* provide us with a similar level of abstraction: as we built priority queues and heapsort, we didn't care *how* the procedures worked, but we knew *what* they did (fixing an array with the *Heap* property broken at one end or the other). Good engineering allowed us to define these black-box components once, and then use them to assemble two different kinds of systems.

Abstract Data Types. Built-in data types in programming languages are abstractly defined by means of a mathematical object and operations on the object, together with certain limitations; users needn't know about their implementation. The "dictionaries" in Section 11.3 and the priority queues of this column can be viewed in the same way.

PROPERTY	INTEGERS	PRIORITY QUEUES	DICTIONARIES
Mathematical Model	Integer	Set of Integers	Set of Integers
Operations	Assignment, Addition, etc.	Initialize to empty, *Insert*, *ExtractMin*	Initialize to empty, *Insert, Member*, *PrintInOrder*
Limitations	Maximum and minimum size	Maximum set size, Size of elements	Maximum set size, Size of elements
Implementations	Two's complement, Signed decimal	Sorted array, Heap	Bit vectors, Bins, Arrays, Trees

Some modern programming languages allow programmers to define their own data types, such as priority queues. Subsequent code may declare a variable to be of type "Priority Queue"; the code sees only the abstraction, and may not know about its implementation. Such a program is illustrated in Solution 10; the discipline increases the ease of re-using software.

12.6 Problems

1. Modify *SiftDown* to have the following specification.

```
proc SiftDown(L,U)
        pre    Heap(L+1,U)
        post   Heap(L,U)
```

What is the run time of the code? Show how it can be used to construct an N-element heap in $O(N)$ time and thereby a faster Heapsort that also uses less code.

2. Implement Heapsort to run as quickly as possible. How does it compare to sorting algorithms tabulated in Section 10.3? Implement heap-based priority queues to run as quickly as possible; at what values of N are they superior to sequential structures?

3. How might the heap implementation of priority queues be used to solve the following problems? How do your answers change when the inputs are sorted?

   a. Construct a Huffman code (such codes are discussed in most books on information theory and many books on data structures).

   b. Compute the sum of a large set of floating point numbers.

   c. Find the 1000 largest of ten million numbers stored on a magnetic tape.

   d. Merge many small sorted files into one large sorted file (this problem arises in implementing a disk-based merge sort program like that in Section 1.3).

4. [D. S. Johnson] The bin packing problem calls for assigning a set of N

weights (each between zero and one) to a minimal number of unit-capacity bins. The first-fit heuristic for this problem considers the weights in the sequence in which they are presented, and places each weight in the first bin in which it fits, scanning the bins in increasing order. Show how a heap-like structure can implement this heuristic in $O(N \log N)$ time. (This problem is distantly related to efficient algorithms for first-fit storage allocation, such as those discussed in Exercise 6.2.4.30 of Knuth's *Sorting and Searching*.)

5. [E. McCreight] A common implementation of sequential files on disk has each block point to its successor, which may be any block on the disk. This method requires a constant amount of time to write a block (as the file is originally written), to read the first block in the file, and to read the Ith block, once you have read the $I-1^{st}$ block. Reading the Ith block from scratch therefore requires time proportional to I. Show how by adding just one additional pointer per node, you can keep all the other properties, but allow the Ith block to be read in time proportional to $\log I$. Explain what the algorithm for reading the Ith block has in common with the code in Problem 4.9 for raising a number to the Ith power in time proportional to $\log I$.

6. On many computers the most expensive part of a binary search program is the division by 2 to find the center of the current range. Show how to replace that division with a multiplication, assuming that the table has been constructed properly. Give algorithms for building and searching such a table.

7. What are appropriate implementations for a priority queue that represents integers in the range $1..K$, when the average size of the set is much larger than K?

8. Prove that the simultaneous logarithmic run times of *Insert* and *ExtractMin* in the heap implementation of priority queues are within a constant factor of optimal.

9. The basic idea of heaps is familiar to sports fans. Suppose that Brian beat Al and Lynn beat Peter in the semifinals, and Lynn triumphed over Brian in the championship match. Those results are usually drawn as

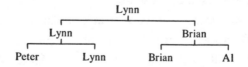

Such "tournament trees" are common in tennis tournaments and in post-season playoffs in football, baseball and basketball. Assuming that the results of matches are consistent (an assumption often invalid in athletics), what is the probability that the second-best player is in the championship match? Give an algorithm for "seeding" the players according to their pre-tournament rankings.

10. Implement heaps in a language that supports abstract data types.

12.7 Further Reading

J. W. J. Williams's original paper on heaps appeared in the June 1964 *Communications of the ACM* and is still fascinating reading today. Even though it is miniature by today's standards (less than a page long), it is large by the standards of the time (Floyd's *TREESORT* algorithm in the August 1962 *CACM* was less than a quarter of a page).

For a more up-to-date view of heaps, see Tarjan's *Data Structures and Network Algorithms*, published in 1983 by the Society for Industrial and Applied Mathematics. This monograph is a fine introduction to the field described in its title; Chapter 3 is devoted to heaps.

COLUMN 13: **A SPELLING CHECKER**

Spelling misteaks irritate readers. And for most writers, checking spelling is a boring and error-prone job. Fortunately, the problem is ideally suited for computers: dull, repetitive work that requires fast reading and a good memory.

In this column we'll study the design of the UNIX system's spelling checker spell. It's a beautiful and useful program, with a history rich in important lessons about program development.

13.1 A Simple Program

Steve Johnson wrote the first version of spell in an afternoon in 1975. His approach is straightforward: isolate the words in a document, sort them, and then compare the sorted list with the dictionary.

The output is a list of all words in the document that aren't in the dictionary. If you meant to write *stationary*, this process will catch the misspelling *stationiry* but not *stationery*, because the latter is a valid word.

Kernighan and Plauger reconstruct Johnson's program on page 133 of their *Software Tools in Pascal*. Their pipeline of programs can be paraphrased as

```
prepare filename |      # remove formatting commands
translit A-Z a-z |      # map upper to lower case
translit ^a-z \n |      # remove punctuation
sort |                  # put words in alphabetical order
unique |                # remove duplicate words
common -2 dict          # report words not in dictionary
```

The vertical bar connects the output of one program with the input to the next program. The input to the first program is filename, and the output of the last program is the list of (potentially) misspelled words.

139

The first program in the pipeline, `prepare`, deals with the formatting commands in many computerized documents. To print a word in a **boldface** font, for instance, one might type @b(boldface) or \fBboldface\fR. A spelling checker must ignore such commands; the poor user who wades through misspellings like *b* and *fbboldface* is too exhausted to notice real errors. `prepare` copies its input to its output, with formatting commands removed.

`translit` transliterates its input to its output, substituting certain characters. Its first invocation in the pipeline changes upper case letters to lower case. The next invocation removes all nonalphabetic characters by mapping them into the newline character, \n. The result is a file that contains the words of the document in the order they appear, with at most one word per line (many lines are empty).

The next program `sorts` the words into alphabetic order, and `unique` removes multiple occurrences. The result is a sorted list of the distinct words in the document. `common`, with the cryptic -2 option, uses a standard merge algorithm to report all lines in its (sorted) input that are not in the (sorted) named file, and the output is the desired list of spelling errors.

In an afternoon Johnson assembled five existing programs and an online dictionary to make a new tool. His program was far from perfect, but it demonstrated the feasibility of a spelling checker and gained a loyal following of users. Changes to the program over the next several months were minor modifications to this structure; a complete redesign would have to wait for several years.

13.2 The Design Space

Before moving on to the next version of `spell`, let's survey the options available to a designer. We'll first examine the program's external appearance (the problem specification seen by the user), and then turn to the program's internal structure.

When hunting for bogus words, it can be helpful to know their source: bad spelling or bad typing. Poor spellers often write *oftun*, good spellers occasionally write *occaisionally*, and we all make *typnig* mistakes. The design of a program may reflect the errors its users make most frequently.

There are two mistakes a spelling program can make, and both compromise its usefulness. Failing to flag an illegal word is an obvious problem. And if a program reports too many valid words as errors, the user may be unwilling to search through the mud to find the pay dirt. All spelling programs make mistakes — whether to report too few or too many suspicious words is a difficult design choice.

The program should check words for spelling, but what exactly is a word? Johnson's checker recognized the importance of removing formatting commands. It ignored distinctions between upper and lower case, and therefore correctly looked up *The* as *the*. Some case problems are more subtle: *DEC* is the name of a computer company and *Dec* is a month, but *dec* is an error (unless, of course, it is an abbreviation for decimal). Other subtleties about words include numbers, hyphens and apostrophes (consider *VAX-11/780* and *his's*). A prototype can be sloppy about these fine points, but a production program should be more careful.

And what about the dictionary itself? A program should recognize some words not in a regular dictionary, such as *IBM* and *VLSI* (but not *vlsi*). But bigger isn't always better — the dictionary may know that a *cere* is near a bird's bill, but in one of my files it is more likely a misspelling of *care*. An affix is a prefix like *pre-* or a suffix like *-ly*; most dictionaries leave affix analysis to the reader. Although a spelling checker may in good conscience report *antidisestablishmentarianism* as a mistake, I would be miffed to wade through a long list of misspellings like *cats* and *replay* when *cat* and *play* were in the dictionary. Johnson modified his program to handle the common *-s* and *-ed* endings, but a production spelling checker must do a more thorough job of affix analysis.

Perhaps the most debated problem in specifying a spelling program is what it should do when it finds an error. Johnson's simple checker produces a list of misspelled words. At the other extreme, interactive spelling *correctors* show the user a misspelled word in its context and ask whether to leave the word unchanged, change this occurrence to a suggested word, change this and all future occurrences to the suggested word, edit this word and change all future occurrences to the edited version, and so on and so on.

Some people say they couldn't live without a fancy spelling corrector — poor spellers seem to find its advice especially valuable. My personal taste, as a fairly good speller, runs towards a simple checker. I now routinely use `spell` on all documents; I rarely used the fancy corrector on a previous system because it took several minutes for me to relearn its command language each time I tried it. Its advice was often more irritating (or amusing) than helpful — it once suggested that J. W. Tukey's last name be corrected to "Turkey". Additionally, a corrector is usually more difficult to build and to maintain than a checker.

Turning from specification to implementation, the two canonical structures for spelling programs are old friends from Section 5.2. Johnson's batch checker used the structure on the left in the figure on the next page; the online program on the right looks up each word as it is encountered.

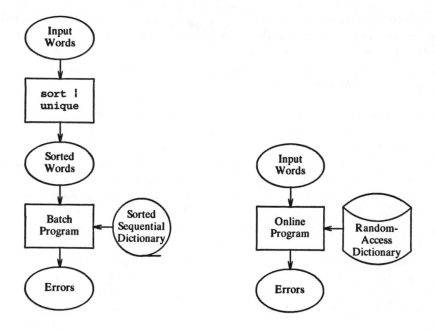

A spelling checker may use either structure, but an interactive corrector is usually restricted to be online. Similarly, a random-access dictionary may be used by either structure, but a sequential dictionary is suitable only for use by a batch program.

There is a tradeoff between sophisticated affix analysis and dictionary size. A simple program that does no affix analysis requires a huge dictionary, including *test*, *tests*, *tested*, *tester*, *testing*, *retest*, *pretest*, etc. Sophisticated affix schemes compress data by storing the single stem *test* along with information that describes its valid affixes. Such schemes may, however, preclude using a sequential dictionary, because *predominant* must be looked up as though it begins with *d* while *invisible* is looked up under *v*.

There are many ways to store the dictionary itself. If it fits in main memory, one should consider using the structures in Section 11.3. The method of choice might be a hash table, a binary search tree, or perhaps a "digital search trie" structure that exploits the fact that a word is a sequence of characters. If the dictionary must reside on disk, then a B-tree or disk hash table may be suitable.

The best implementation of the dictionary depends on several factors. A simple data structure will ease development and maintenance, but a back-of-the-envelope calculation shows that performance may be crucial in this application. Suppose that a disk-based scheme looks up a word in two disk reads of fifty milliseconds each. The program processes ten words per second, so a document of four thousand words (the average size of these columns) requires six long minutes. The program we'll soon study does the job in half a minute.† A spelling corrector referenced in Section 13.6 sometimes makes as many as 200 disk accesses to correct a single misspelled word, which translates to ten seconds and an annoying wait for the on-line user.

The following outline sketches our considerations of the design space; Problem 4 mentions approaches to spelling programs that are outside this space.

REQUIREMENTS — The Customer's View
Typical user
    Source of errors: bad spelling or sloppy typing
    Response to errors: good spellers need only notification
        of their mistakes, bad spellers appreciate more assistance
Development resources
    How much programmer time is available?
Application resources
    Time and space requirements of the final code

SPECIFICATION — The User's View
Word definition
    Fine points include formatting commands, upper vs. lower
        case distinction, and embedded numbers and punctuation
The word list
    Explicit words stored in the list
    Implicit words: present by affix analysis
Response to errors
    Checkers report errors, correctors fix them

IMPLEMENTATION — The Programmer's View
Program structure
    Batch programs sort the words to remove duplicates
    Online programs check each word as it occurs
Word list implementation
    Tradeoffs between affix analysis, dictionary size,
        and quality of answers
Dictionary specification
    Are words accessed in sorted order or random order?
Dictionary implementation
    Primary memory: hashing, search trees, search tries
    Secondary memory: B-trees, hashing
    Combinations store common words in primary memory
        and rarer words on secondary memory

---

† Anecdotal evidence that performance matters: After writing this paragraph I ran McIlroy's spell on the two-thousand-word draft, and twenty seconds later the error list reported the words *monograph*, *textfile*, and *filename*. I fixed the spelling error, and changed several occurrences of *textfile* to *filename* for consistency. That was high return on an investment of twenty seconds; I probably wouldn't have run the program if it cost three minutes.

13.3 A Subtle Program

In this section we'll study the `spell` program that Doug McIlroy wrote in 1978. Its user interface is the same as Johnson's: typing `spell filename` produces a list of the misspelled words in the file. The two advantages of this program over Johnson's are a superior word list and reduced run time. I'm an enthusiastic user: the program is simple to use, and it quickly reports all my misspellings and very few words that aren't in error. My dictionary defines a pearl as something "very choice or precious"; this program qualifies.

The first problem McIlroy faced was assembling the word list; to appreciate some of the subtleties of the task, see Section 13.7. He started by intersecting an unabridged dictionary (for validity) with the million-word Brown University corpus (for currency). That was a reasonable beginning, but there was much work left to do.

McIlroy's approach is illustrated in his quest for proper nouns, which are omitted from most dictionaries. First came people: the 1000 most common last names in a large telephone directory, a list of boys' and girls' names, famous names (like Dijkstra and Nixon), and mythological names from an index to Bulfinch. After observing "misspellings" like *Xerox* and *Texaco*, he added companies on the Fortune 500 list. Publishing companies are rampant in bibliographies, so they're in. Next came geography: the nations and their capitals, the states and theirs, the hundred largest cities in the United States and in the world, and don't forget oceans, planets and stars.

He also added common names of animals and plants, and terms from chemistry, anatomy and (for local consumption) computing. But he was careful not to add too much: he kept out valid words that tend to be real-life misspellings (like the geological term *cwm*) and included only one of several alternative spellings (hence *traveling* but not *travelling*).

McIlroy's trick was to examine `spell`'s output on real runs; for some time, it automatically mailed a copy of the output to him. When he spotted a problem, he would apply the broadest possible solution. The result is a fine list of 75,000 words: it includes most of the words I use in my documents, yet still finds my spelling errors.

`spell`'s affix analysis is both necessary and convenient. It's necessary because there is no such thing as a word list for English; a spelling checker must either guess at the derivation of words like *misrepresented* or report as errors a lot of valid English words. Affix analysis has the convenient side effect of reducing the size of the dictionary.

The goal of affix analysis is to reduce *misrepresented* down to *sent*, stripping off *mis-*, *re-*, *pre-*, and *-ed*.† `spell`'s tables contain 40 prefix rules and 30 suffix rules. A "stop list" of 1300 exceptions halts good but incorrect

---

† Even though *represent* doesn't mean "to present again" and *present* doesn't mean "sent beforehand", `spell` uses coincidences to reduce dictionary size.

guesses like reducing *entend* (a misspelling of *intend*) to *en* + *-tend*. This analysis reduces the 75,000 word list to 30,000 words.

McIlroy's program is the same as Johnson's up to the point of looking up words in the dictionary (the common program in the previous pipeline). The new program loops on each word, stripping affixes and looking up the result until it either finds a match or no affixes remain (and the word is declared to be an error). Because affix processing may destroy the sorted order in which the words arrive, the dictionary is accessed in random order.

Back-of-the-envelope analysis showed the importance of keeping the dictionary in main memory. This was particularly hard for McIlroy, who originally wrote this program on a PDP-11 that had a 64-kilobyte address space. The abstract of his paper summarizes his space squeezing: "Stripping prefixes and suffixes reduces the list below one third of its original size, hashing discards 60 percent of the bits that remain, and data compression halves it once again." Thus a list of 75,000 English words (and roughly as many inflected forms) was represented in 26,000 16-bit computer words.

McIlroy used hashing to represent 30,000 English words in 27 bits each (we'll see later why 27 is magic). We'll study a progression of schemes illustrated on the toy word list

a list of five words

The first hashing method uses an N-element hash table roughly the size of the list and a hash function that maps a string into an integer in the range $1..N$. The Ith entry of the table points to a linked list that contains all strings that hash to I. If null lists are represented by empty cells and the hash function yields $H(a)=3$, $H(list)=2$, etc., then a five-element table might look like

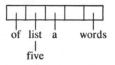

To look up the word W we perform a sequential search in the list pointed to by the $H(W)^{th}$ cell.

The next scheme uses a much larger table. Choosing $N=23$ makes it likely that most hash cells contain just one element. In this example, $H(a)=14$ and $H(list)=6$.

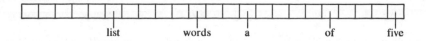

The spell program uses $N=2^{27}$ (roughly 134 million), and all but a few of the non-empty lists contain just a single element.

The next step is daring: instead of a linked list of words, McIlroy stores just a single bit in each table entry. This reduces space dramatically, but introduces errors. This picture uses the same hash function as the previous example, and represents zero bits by empty cells.

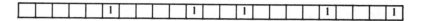

To look up word W, the program accesses the $H(W)^{th}$ bit in the table. If that bit is zero, then the program correctly reports that word W is not in the table. If the bit is one, then the program assumes W is in the table. Sometimes a bad word just happens to hash to a valid bit, but the probability of such an error is just $30,000/2^{27}$, or roughly $1/4,000$. On the average, therefore, one out of every 4000 bad words will sneak by as valid. McIlroy observed that typical rough drafts rarely contain more than 20 errors, so this defect hampers at most one run of spell out of every hundred — that's why he chose 27.

Representing the hash table by a string of $N=2^{27}$ bits would consume over sixteen million bytes. The program therefore represents just the one bits; in the above example,

$$6 \ 11 \ 14 \ 19 \ 23$$

The word W is declared to be in the table if $H(W)$ is present. The obvious representation of those values uses 30,000 27-bit words, but McIlroy's machine had only 32,000 16-bit words in its address space. He therefore sorted the list and used a variable-length code to represent the *differences* between successive hash values. Assuming a fictitious starting value of zero, the above list is compressed to

$$6 \ 5 \ 3 \ 5 \ 4$$

spell represents the differences in an average of 13.6 bits each. That left a few hundred extra words to point at useful starting points in the compressed list and thereby speed up the sequential search. The result is a 64-kilobyte dictionary that has fast access time and almost never makes mistakes.

We've already considered two aspects of spell's performance: it produces useful output and it fits in a 64-kilobyte address space. It's also fast. Solution 2 describes how it can check a 5000-word document in 30 seconds of VAX-11/750 CPU time; that translates into less than 10 minutes for checking this book. To check the spelling of a single word I could type, for instance,

```
spell
necessary
^d
```

and in about four seconds I know that it is valid — the small dictionary can be quickly read from disk. The paper cited in Section 13.6 surveys many spelling programs, but none are in the same performance class as McIlroy's.

13.4 Principles

Here's the story in a nutshell. With a good idea, some powerful tools, and a free afternoon, Steve Johnson built a useful spelling checker in six lines of code. Assured that the project was worthy of substantial effort, a few years later Doug McIlroy spent several months engineering a great program. The tale has several morals.

Prototypes. Before you build a fancy program, let potential users experiment with a simple prototype on many real inputs. Johnson used a trivial word list to build a slow checker; users wanted a better word list and faster program, but there was no demand for a corrector. Prototypes can help estimate parameters of the final product: experience with Johnson's program gave McIlroy insight into the typical number of total, distinct and misspelled words in a document.

Separation of Concerns. A well-built system is divided into independent components, each of which does one thing well. The five different programs in Johnson's pipeline solve five different problems; any one could be enhanced without adversely affecting the others. Affix analysis and dictionary representation are largely independent in McIlroy's program; one needn't learn much about one to work on the other. And for my money, separation of concerns speaks against spelling correctors: errors should be found by a simple checker, fixing them is the job of a text editor, and help about the correct spelling of a word should come from a "suggester" (see Problem 5).

Simplicity. The best design is usually the simplest. Johnson's problem definition is trivial to specify, and his program is clearly described in just a few lines of code. Even McIlroy's subtle data structure yields simplicity: his single dictionary structure performs a function that many programs use several data structures to do more slowly.

Software Engineering. Although it didn't require any formal project management, the `spell` program represents engineering of the first rank. Johnson and McIlroy used the old engineering tools of prototyping, simplicity, separating concerns, careful problem definition and back-of-the-envelope calculations. They built with standard components: the design uses off-the-shelf filters for removing formatting commands, sorting, and removing duplicates. When they couldn't use existing software tools, they used proven techniques: the word list data structure combines hashing, approximation algorithms, and data compression. The final program is steeped in skillful design decisions: McIlroy traded small chunks of run time, space, accuracy, and problem definition to yield an effective tool.

13.5 Problems

1. Gather data on documents and dictionaries such as the distribution of word lengths and the frequency of all possible letters and digrams (letter pairs). For dictionaries, evaluate the compression of simple affix analysis (what percent of words are covered by -s, -ed, and -ly?). For documents, count the number of total, distinct and misspelled words. What other statistics are useful to know?

2. Use back-of-the-envelope calculations to evaluate various designs for a spelling checker. (For instance, should a fast filter be used to weed out the one hundred most common English words? Is it worth sorting the words to remove duplicates in a batch program that uses a fast online dictionary?) Characterize the run time of the spelling program on your system.

3. Investigate other data structures for random-access dictionaries. Consider especially structures that don't always give the right answer. Analyze space requirements and run time (both for reading the dictionary from disk and for accessing a word).

4. Investigate spelling checkers that don't use a complete dictionary.

5. Design a spelling suggester that a bad speller might use with a checker. Given the input *occurrance*, it should suggest that you mean *occurrence*.

6. Programs for checking spelling, playing word games, and making crossword puzzles require different dictionaries. Give words that might be in one of the dictionaries but not in the others. What other dictionaries might be required by various programs?

7. Discuss the design of spelling checkers for languages other than English. In connexion with this problem, how would a programme check spelling of the British flavour?

8. Discuss the specification and implementation of other programs that might prove useful to writers who store their documents on computers.

9. Design a program for finding the K most common words in an input file, where K is typically around 100.

10. The errors inherent in McIlroy's approximate dictionary are acceptable for his spelling checker — it only accepts an invalid word in one percent of the runs. How does it fare in other contexts, such as the spelling suggester in Problem 5 or in programs that play word games?

13.6 Further Reading

The details of McIlroy's `spell` program are in his paper "Development of a spelling list" in *IEEE Transactions on Communications COM-30*, 1 (January 1982, pp. 91-99). It is fascinating and delightful reading, and a must for any serious student of programming.

"Computer programs for detecting and correcting spelling errors" by James L. Peterson appeared in the December 1980 *Communications of the ACM*. The first part of the paper surveys the spelling problem and various implementations of checkers and correctors. He then describes a spelling corrector that he designed and implemented; the complete Pascal program is published in a Springer-Verlag monograph. The paper's 44 references are an excellent introduction to the literature of spelling.

13.7 Why Spelling is Hard *[Sidebar]*

The recipe for elephant stew begins, "First, catch an elephant." If your recipe for building a spelling program begins, "First, find a valid word list for English", you may find it easier to prepare a delicious dish of elephant stew. After reading a draft of this column, Vic Vyssotsky wrote the following note, which helped me appreciate the problem.

"Spelling is one of the best examples I've seen of the need for prototyping: build something small, try it, see how useful it is in practice, then modify and extend. As you point out, it would be nearly impossible to guess a priori what features a spelling checker should have in detail in order to be most useful.

"This is related to the fact that we're dealing with English. French, for instance, has an academy to define root words and a more systematic set of derivations. In French it is a great deal easier than in English to determine whether *glotchification* is a word and is correctly spelled. So it would be much easier to build a spelling checker for French than for English. But it would also be much less useful for French, because anybody who writes much in French knows how to spell correctly (and how to determine word boundaries, and how to decide whether a particular neologism is plausible).

"Language has the challenging property of changing as we speak: *fribble* is a word, and it's in Webster's, but my daughters would be astonished at the dictionary's definition; *glotch* is a word, and everybody knows what it means†, but it's not in Webster's; *glout* is clearly not a word, Webster's notwithstanding. These days I encounter *cwm* more often than *cum* (because climbing has become a popular sport, and children are no longer forced to learn Latin), but thirty years ago it was the other way around. And what's the correct spelling of *thru*? A generation ago, grade school teachers knew the answer, even if I didn't, but the California Department of Highways changed it for all of us.

"It seems to me that this malleability of English is the deep fundamental reason why a spelling corrector won't work. My fifth grade English teacher was a spelling corrector, and in your draft column she would surely correct *newline* and *online* as well as *filename*, none of which need correcting. I still remember the firmness of the putdown she administered when I suggested adding *abaft* to her canonical list of all-the-prepositions-in-the-English-

---
† I didn't — a glotch is a large, disorderly aggregate.

language. Unfortunately for correctors, whether human or electronic, the English language (and its spelling) rests on agreement among its users, and not on decisions made by an academy of experts.

"That's what makes a spelling checker such an interesting undertaking, and such a good example of program design issues."

EPILOG

An interview with the author seemed to be the best conclusion for this book, so here goes.

Q: Thanks for agreeing to do this interview.
A: No problem — my time is your time.

Q: Seeing how these columns already appeared in *Communications of the ACM*, why did you bother to collect them into a book?
A: There are several little reasons: I've fixed dozens of errors, made hundreds of little improvements, and added several new sections. There are fifty percent more problems, solutions, and pictures in the book. Also, it's more convenient to have the columns in one book rather than a dozen magazines. The big reason, though, is that the themes running through the columns are easier to see when they are collected together; the whole is greater than the sum of the parts.

Q: What are those themes?
A: The most important is that thinking hard about programming can be both useful and fun. There's more to the job than systematic program development from formal requirements documents. If this book helps just one disillusioned programmer to fall back in love with his or her work, it will have served its purpose.

Q: That's a pretty fluffy answer. Are there technical threads tying the columns together?
A: Performance is the topic of Part II, and a theme that runs through all columns. Program verification is used extensively in several columns. The Appendix catalogs the algorithms in the book.

Q: It seems that most columns emphasize the design process. Can you summarize your advice on that topic?
A: I'm glad you asked. I just happened to prepare a list before this interview. Here are some points that occur repeatedly in "Principles" sections.

151

Work on the right problem.
Explore the design space of solutions.
Look at the data.
Use the back of the envelope.
Design with components.
Build prototypes.
Make tradeoffs when you have to.
Keep it simple.

The points were originally discussed in the context of programming, but they apply to any engineering endeavor.

Q: That raises a point that has bothered me: it's easy to simplify the little programs in this book, but do the techniques scale up to real software?

A: I have three answers: yes, no, and maybe. Yes they scale up; Section 3.4, for instance, describes a huge software project that was simplified down to "just" 80 staff-years. An equally trite answer is no: if you simplify properly, you avoid building jumbo systems and the techniques don't need to scale up. Although there is merit in both views, the truth lies somewhere in between, and that's where the maybe comes in. Some software has to be big, and the themes of this book are sometimes applicable to such systems. The UNIX system is a fine example of a powerful whole built out of simple and elegant parts.

Q: There you go talking about another Bell Labs system. Aren't these columns a little too parochial?

A: Maybe a little. I've stuck to material that I've seen used in practice, and that biases the book towards my environment. Phrased more positively, much of the material in these columns was contributed by my colleagues, and they deserve the credit (or blame). I've learned a lot from many researchers and developers within Bell Labs. There's a fine corporate atmosphere that encourages interaction between research and development. So a lot of what you call parochialism is just my enthusiasm for my employer.

Q: Let's come back down to earth. Why do you use so many different languages? The book is littered with AWK, BASIC, C, COBOL, FORTRAN, and your own weird pseudocode based on Pascal. Why not just choose the one best language and stick with it?

A: The ideas in this book aren't limited to any one programming language. Programmers should learn to think in a convenient pseudocode, and then express their ideas in the implementation language. David Gries said it best: program *into* a language, not *in* it.

Q: What pieces are missing from this book?

A: The spelling checker in Column 13 is the largest program described in detail. I had hoped to include a large system composed of many programs, but

I couldn't describe any interesting systems in the ten or so pages of a typical column. Readers interested in such systems should see the "Case Studies" department of *Communications of the ACM*, which first appeared in the July 1984 issue.

At a more general level, I'd like to do future *CACM* columns on the themes of "computer science for programmers" (like program verification in Column 4 and algorithm design in Column 7) and the "engineering techniques of computing" (like the back-of-the-envelope calculations in Column 6).

Q: If you're so into "science" and "engineering", how come the columns are so light on theorems and tables and so heavy on stories?

A: Watch it — people who interview themselves shouldn't criticize writing styles.

APPENDIX: CATALOG OF ALGORITHMS

This book covers much of the material in a college algorithms course, but from a different perspective — the emphasis is more on applications and coding than on mathematical analysis. This appendix relates the material to a more typical outline.

Sorting

Problem Definition. The output sequence is an ordered permutation of the input sequence. When the input is a disk file, the output is usually a distinct disk file; when the input is an array, the output is usually the same array.

Applications. This list only hints at the diversity of sorting applications.

- Output Requirements. Some users desire sorted output; see Section 1.1 and consider your telephone directory and monthly checking account statement. Routines such as binary search require sorted inputs.

- Collect Equal Items. Programmers use sorting to collect together the equal items in a sequence: Johnson's spelling checker in Section 13.1 collects the words in a document and the anagram program in Sections 2.4 and 2.8 collects words in the same anagram class. The sorted input files in Sections 5.2 and 13.1 allow equal elements to be processed by merging. See also Problems 2.6, 7.4, and 13.4.

- Other Applications. The anagram program in Sections 2.4 and 2.8 uses sorting as a canonical order for the letters in a word, and thereby as a signature of an anagram class. Problem 2.7 sorts to rearrange data on a tape.

General-Purpose Routines. The following routines sort an arbitrary N-element sequence.

- Insertion Sort. The five-line program in Section 10.1 has $O(N^2)$ run time in the worst case and for random inputs. In Section 10.2 it is used to sort an almost sorted array in $O(N)$ time. It is the only *stable* sort in this book: output elements with equal keys are in the same relative order as in the input. Solution 8.10 contains a C implementation.

155

- Quicksort. The 12-line Quicksort in Section 10.2 runs in $O(N \log N)$ expected time on an array of N distinct elements. It is recursive and uses logarithmic stack space on the average. In the worst case, it requires $O(N^2)$ time and $O(N)$ stack space. It runs in $O(N^2)$ time on an array of equal elements; the 15-line version in Problem 10.3 has $O(N \log N)$ average run time for *any* array (Problem 10.11 proposes an alternative scheme). Problem 10.13 suggests a better partitioning element. The table in Section 10.3 and the Solutions 8.10 and 10.10 present empirical data on the run time of Quicksort. Solution 8.10 contains a C implementation.

- Heapsort. The Heapsort in Section 12.4 runs in $O(N \log N)$ time on any N-element array; it is not recursive and uses only constant extra space. Solutions 12.1 and 12.2 describe a faster Heapsort in just 14 lines of code.

- Mergesort. The algorithm sketched in Section 1.3 is effective for sorting disk and tape files. A merging algorithm is sketched in Problem 12.3.d.

The run times of Insertion Sort and Quicksort are compared in Section 10.3; the run times of other sorting algorithms are discussed in Solution 1.3.

Special-Purpose Routines. These routines lead to short and efficient programs for certain inputs.

- Radix Sort. McIlroy's bit-string sort in Problem 10.6 can be generalized to sort strings over larger alphabets (bytes, for instance).

- Bitmap Sort. The seven-line bitmap sort in Section 1.4 used the fact that the integers to be sorted were from a small range, contained no duplicates, and had no additional data. Implementation details and extensions are described in Problems 1.2 and 1.5.

- Other Sorts. The multiple-pass sort in Section 1.3 reads the input many times to trade time for space. Section 11.1 describes the problem of generating a sorted list of random integers; programs are given in Sections 11.2 and 11.3.

Searching

Problem Definition. A search routine determines whether its input is a member of a given set, and possibly retrieves associated information. In *static* applications the set is known before any searches are performed; in *dynamic* applications elements can be inserted into the set and deleted from the set.

Applications. Lesk's telephone directory in Problem 2.6 searches to convert an (encoded) name to a telephone number. Thompson's endgame program in Section 9.7 searches a set of chess boards to compute an optimal move. McIlroy's spelling checker in Section 13.3 searches a dictionary to determine whether a word is spelled correctly. Additional applications are described along with the routines.

General-Purpose Routines. The following routines search an arbitrary *N*-element set.

- Sequential Search. The code for searching an array is given in Problem 4.9; a faster version is in Problem 8.5. The algorithm is used in hyphenating words (Problem 3.5), smoothing geographic data (Section 8.2), representing a sparse matrix (Section 9.2), generating random sets (Section 11.3), and bin packing (Problem 12.4). The introduction to Column 3 and Problem 3.1 describe two foolish programs that implement sequential search.

- Binary Search. The algorithm to search a sorted array in $O(\log N)$ comparisons is described in Section 2.2, and code is developed in Section 4.2. Section 8.3 extends the code to find the first occurrence of many equal items and tunes its performance; a more efficient data structure is described in Problem 12.6. Applications include searching for anagrams of an input word (Problem 2.1), telephone numbers (Problem 2.6), the position of a point among line segments (Problem 4.7), the index of an entry in a sparse array (Problem 9.2), and a random integer (Section 11.3). The applications in Problem 12.3 use a binary search on a heap data structure. Problems 2.9 and 8.7 discuss the tradeoffs between binary and sequential search.

- Other Methods. Problem 1.9 hashes telephone numbers, Section 11.3 hashes a set of integers, and Section 13.3 hashes the words in a dictionary (see also Problem 13.3). Section 11.3 sketches binary search trees. Speedups to these routines are described in Problem 8.6.

Special-Purpose Routines. These routines lead to short and efficient programs for certain inputs.

- Key Indexing. Some keys can be used as an index into an array of values. Keys used as indices include precinct numbers (Section 1.4), college course numbers (Problem 1.7), characters (Section 8.2), arguments to trigonometric functions (Problem 8.9), indices of sparse arrays (Section 9.2), program counter values (Problem 9.7), chess boards (Section 9.7), random integers (Section 11.3), and values in priority queues (Problem 12.7). Problem 8.4 reduces space with key indexing and a numerical function.

- Other Methods. Section 8.1 describes how search time was reduced by keeping common elements in a cache. Section 9.1 describes how searching a tax table became simple once the context was understood.

Other Set Algorithms

These problems deal with a collection of *N* elements that may possibly contain duplicates.

Selection. Problem 2.8 describes a problem in which we must select the Kth-smallest element in the set. Solution 10.9 describes an efficient algorithm for the task; slower algorithms are mentioned in Problems 2.8, 10.1 and 12.3.c.

Priority Queues. A priority queue maintains a set of elements under the operations of inserting arbitrary elements and deleting the minimum element. Section 12.3 describes two sequential structures for the task. The heaps described in that section are particularly efficient. Applications are described in Problems 12.3, 12.4 and 12.7. Solution 12.10 contains a C++ program.

Vector and Matrix Algorithms

Algorithms for swapping subsequences of a vector are discussed in Section 2.3 and Problems 2.3 and 2.4; Solution 2.3 contains code for the algorithms. Programs for computing the maximum of a vector are described in Problems 4.9 and 8.6. Problem 2.7 uses sorting to transpose a matrix represented on tape. Vector and matrix algorithms that share space are described in Sections 9.2 and 12.4. Sparse vectors and matrices are discussed in Sections 3.1, 9.2 and 13.3; Problem 1.8 describes a scheme for initializing sparse vectors that is used in Section 11.3. Column 7 describes five algorithms for computing the maximum-sum subsequence in a vector, and several of the problems in Column 7 deal with vectors and matrices.

Random Objects

Routines for generating pseudorandom reals and integers are specified and used in Section 10.2 and 11.1   Section 11.3 describes an algorithm for "shuffling" the elements of an array. Sections 11.1 through 11.3 describe several algorithms for selecting random subsets of a set (see also Problem 11.6); Problem 1.4 gives an application of this algorithm.

Other Algorithms

Section 7.9 surveys the impact of algorithms on problems in numerical analysis, graphs, and geometry.

Numeric Algorithms Solution 2.3 presents the additive Euclidean algorithm for computing the greates common divisor of two integers. Problem 4.9 gives code for an efficient algorithm to raise a number to a positive integer power. Problem 8.9 computes trigonometric functions by table lookup. Solution 8.11 describes Horner's method of evaluating a polynomial. Summing a large set of floating point numbers is described in Problems 10.1 and 12.3.

Databases. Section 3.4 sketches the entity-relationship database used in a large software system. Problem 1.9 describes how hashing is used in a department store's database implemented using paper forms.

HINTS FOR SELECTED PROBLEMS

Column 1

1. Consider a two-pass algorithm.

4. Read Column 11.

5, 7, 8. Try key indexing.

9. Consider hashing, and don't limit yourself to a computerized system.

10. This problem is for the birds.

Column 2

1. Think about sorting, binary search, and signatures.

2. Strive for an algorithm that runs in linear time.

4. Consider the effect of paging.

5. Exploit the identity $CBA = (A^R B^R C^R)^R$.

7. Vyssotsky used a system program and two simple programs to reformat data on tapes.

8. Consider the K smallest elements in the set.

9. The cost of S sequential searches is proportional to SN; the total cost of S binary searches is the cost of the searches plus the time required to sort the table. Before you put too much faith in the constant factors of the various algorithms, see Problem 8.7.

10. How did Archimedes determine that the king's crown wasn't pure gold?

Column 3

2. Use one array to represent the coefficients of the recurrence and another to represent the k previous values. The program consists of a loop within a loop.

4. Only one routine need be written from scratch; the other two can use that as a subroutine.

6. An AWK program for the task required just twelve lines of code. It didn't follow the outline in Section 3.2, but rather used AWK's arrays, input fields, and substring substitution facilities.

Column 4

2. Work from a precise invariant. Consider adding two dummy elements to the array to help you initialize your invariant: $X[0]=-\infty$ and $X[N+1]=\infty$.

5. If you solve this problem, run to the nearest mathematics department and ask for a Ph.D.

6. Look for an invariant preserved by the process, and relate the initial condition of the can to its terminal condition.

7. Read Section 2.2 again.

9. Try the following loop invariants, which are true immediately before the test in the while statement. For vector addition,

$$I \le N+1 \quad \text{and} \quad \forall_{1 \le j \le I-1} A[j] = B[j]+C[j]$$

and for sequential search,

$$I \le N+1 \quad \text{and} \quad \forall_{1 < j \le I-1} X[j] \ne T$$

Column 5

2. Try working on Conway's Game of Life at the following design levels. Problem definition: how large is the board? what is the output of the program? Algorithms: can you find a way to keep track of the currently active region of the board? can you detect cycles? Data structures: should the board be represented by a sparse array, a regular two-dimensional array, or a combination? Code tuning and hardware: I've seen microcoded Games of Life run like the wind.

7. Automobile accidents are avoided by measures such as driver training, strict enforcement of speed limits, a minimum drinking age, stiff penalties for drunk driving, and a good system of public transportation. If accidents do occur, injuries to passengers can be reduced by the design of the passenger compartment, wearing seat belts (perhaps as mandated by law), and air bags. And if injuries are suffered, their effect can be reduced by paramedics at the scene, rapid evacuation in helicopter ambulances, trauma centers, and corrective surgery.

Column 6

10. Some people are afraid of supplying numbers ("I have no idea how deep the Mississippi River is"). At the other extreme are people who gladly supply accuracy that isn't there ("the river is 31.415926535 feet deep").

Column 7

4, 5, 6. Use a cumulative array.

7. The obvious algorithm has $O(N^4)$ run time; strive for a cubic algorithm.

8. In addition to computing the maximum sum in the region, return information about the maximum vectors ending at each side of the array.

Column 8

1. Assume that each byte has eight bits; how can you use them?

2. What is the relationship between *CountTable* [0..7] and *CountTable* [8..15]?

4. Mix and match functions and tables.

7. To make binary search competitive with sequential search even at small values of N, make the comparison operation very expensive (see, for instance, Problem 4.7).

Column 9

1. What code did the compiler generate for accessing packed fields?

4. Encode runs.

7. Reduce the data by considering certain ranges of memory to be equivalent. Those ranges might be either fixed-length blocks (say, 64 bytes) or subroutine boundaries.

Column 10

4. Let the loop index I move from right to left, so that it approaches the known value T in $X[L]$.

5. When you have two subproblems to solve, which should you solve right away and which should you leave on the stack to return to later — larger or smaller?

9. Modify Quicksort so that it recurs only on the subrange that contains K.

Column 11

3. Go to a statistician and use the phrases "coupon collector's test" and "birthday problem".

8. The problem said you *could* use the computer; it didn't say you had to.

Column 12

1. Aim for a Heapsort with this structure.

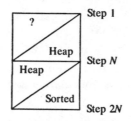

2. See Problem 1, and also consider moving code out of loops.

5. Heaps have implicit pointers from node I to node $2I$; try the same in disk files.

6. Binary search in $X[1..7]$ uses an implicit tree whose root is in $X[4]$. How might the implicit trees of Section 12.1 be used instead?

8. Use the $O(N \log N)$ lower bound on sorting. If both *Insert* and *ExtractMin* run in less than $O(\log N)$ time, then you could sort in less than $O(N \log N)$ time; show how.

Column 13

4. Possible approaches include finding near misses (such as the words *programmer* and *programer* in one document) and checking for common letter pairs and triples (see Problem 1)

9. What aoes this problem have ın commoɒ wıth a speılıng checker˟

SOLUTIONS TO SELECTED PROBLEMS

Solutions for Column 1

1. A two-pass algorithm first sorts the integers 1 through 13,500 using 13,500/16=844 words of storage, then sorts 13,501 through 27,000 in a second pass. A K-pass algorithm sorts at most N nonrepeated integers from $1..N$ in time KN and space N/K.

3. The (finely tuned) system sort took 65 seconds on a VAX-11/750 to sort a file of 26,000 distinct integers from $1..27,000$. My first implementation of the bitmap sort required 41.6 seconds for the same data: 32 seconds in input/output and 9.6 seconds in computation. Tuning the bitmap sort using the principles of Column 8 dropped its runtime to 14 seconds: 12.3 in input/output and 1.7 in computation.

4. See Column 11, especially Problem 11.7. This code assumes that $RandInt(A,B)$ returns a random integer in $A..B$.

```
for I := 1 to N do
    X[I] := I
for I := 1 to K do
    Swap(X[I], X[RandInt(I,N)])
    print X[I]
```

The *RandInt* function is discussed in Section 10.2.

5. If each integer appears at most ten times, then we can count its occurrences in a four-bit half-byte (or nybble). Using the solution to Problem 1, we can sort the complete file in a single pass with 27,000/2 bytes, or in K passes with 27,000/2K bytes.

7. The course information can be represented in 20,000 bytes of main memory by keeping for each possible course number a two-byte count of the number of seats available. If a given four-digit number is not a valid course, then a special value (such as -1) is stored in its position in the 10,000-element table. This change reduced the run time of the proposed program from hours to minutes.

163

8 The effect of initializing the vector $Data[1..N]$ can be accomplished with a signature contained in two additional N-element vectors, $From$ and To, and an integer Top. If the element $Data[I]$ has been initialized, then $From[I] \leq Top$ and $To[From[I]] = I$. Thus $From$ is a simple signature, and To and Top together make sure that $From$ is not accidentally signed by the random contents of memory. Blank entries of $Data$ are uninitialized in this picture:

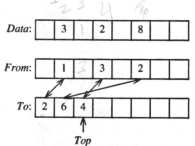

Top is initially zero; the array element I is first accessed by the code

```
Top      := Top+1
From[I]  := Top
To[Top]  := I
Data[I]  := 0
```

This method (due to Aho, Hopcroft and Ullman) cleverly combines key indexing and a wily signature scheme. It can be used for matrices as well as vectors.

9. The store places the paper order forms in a 10×10 array of bins, using the last two digits of the customer's phone number as the hash index. When the customer telephones an order, it is placed in the proper bin. When the customer arrives to retrieve the merchandise, the salesperson sequentially searches through the orders in the appropriate bin — this is classical "open hashing with collision resolution by sequential search". The last two digits of the phone number are quite close to random and therefore an excellent hash function, while the first two digits would be a horrible hash function — why? Some municipalities use a similar scheme to record deeds in sets of record books.

10. The computers at the two facilities were linked by microwave, but printing the drawings at the test base would have required an expensive printer. The team therefore drew the pictures at the main plant, photographed them, and sent 35mm film to the test station by carrier pigeon, where it was enlarged and printed. The pigeon's 45-minute flight took half the time of the car, and cost only a few dollars per day. During the 16 months of the project the pigeons transmitted several hundred rolls of film, and only two were lost (there are hawks in the area; no classified data was carried).

Solutions for Column 2

A. It is helpful to view this binary search in terms of the twenty bits that represent each integer. In the first pass of the algorithm we read the (at most) one million input integers and write those with a leading zero bit to one tape and those with a leading one bit to another tape.

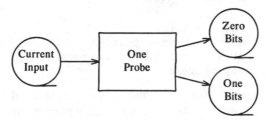

One of those two tapes contains at most 500,000 integers, so we next use that tape as the current input and repeat the probe process, but this time on the second bit. If the original input tape contains N elements, the first pass will read N integers, the second pass at most $N/2$, the third pass at most $N/4$, and so on, so the total running time is proportional to N. The missing integer could be found by sorting on tape and then scanning, but that would require time proportional to $N \log N$. This problem and solution are due to Ed Reingold of the University of Illinois.

B. See Section 2.3.

C. See Section 2.4.

1. To find all anagrams of a given word we first compute its signature. If no preprocessing is allowed then we have to read the entire dictionary sequentially, compute the signature of each word, and compare the two signatures; an array of counts is probably a good signature scheme. With preprocessing, we perform a binary search in a precomputed file containing (signature, word) pairs sorted by signature.

2. Binary search finds an element that occurs at least twice by recursively searching the subinterval that contains more than half of the integers. My original solution did not guarantee that the number of integers is halved in each iteration, so the worst-case run time of its $\log_2 N$ passes was proportional to $N \log N$. Jim Saxe of Carnegie-Mellon University reduced that to linear time by observing that the search can avoid carrying too many duplicates. When his search knows that a duplicate must be in a current range of M integers, it will only store $M+1$ integers on its current work tape; if more integers would have gone on the tape, his program merely discards them. Although his method frequently ignores input variables, its strategy is conservative enough to ensure that it finds at least one duplicate.

3. This "juggling" code rotates $X[1..N]$ left by *RotDist*.

```
for I := 1 to GCD(RotDist,N) do
    /* Move I-th values of blocks */
    This := I
    Temp := X[This]
    Next := This + RotDist
    if Next > N then Next := Next-N
    while Next ≠ I do
        X[This] := X[Next]
        This := Next
        Next := Next + RotDist
        if Next > N then Next := Next-N
    X[This] := Temp
```

The greatest common divisor of *I* and *N* is the number of cycles to be permuted (in terms of modern algebra, it is the number of cosets in the permutation group induced by the rotation). The next program is from Section 18.1 of Gries's *Science of Programming*; it assumes that the subroutine $Swap(A,B,L)$ exchanges $X[A..A+L-1]$ with $X[B..B+L-1]$.

```
P := RotDist+1
I := RotDist; J := N-RotDist
while I ≠ J do
    /* Invariant:
        X[1  ..P-I-1] is in final position
        X[P-I..P-1  ] = A is to be swapped with B
        X[P  ..P+J-1] = B is to be swapped with A
        X[P+J..N    ] is in final position
    */
    if I > J then
        Swap(P-I, P, J);     I := I-J
      else
        Swap(P-I, P+J-I, I); J := J-I
Swap(P-I, P, I)
```

Loop invariants are described in Column 4. The code is isomorphic to the (slow but correct) additive Euclidean algorithm for computing the greatest common divisor of *I* and *J*.

```
function GCD(I,J)
    while I ≠ J
        if I > J then
            I := I-J
          else
            J := J-I
    return I
```

Gries and Mills study all three rotation algorithms in "Swapping Sections", Cornell University Computer Science Technical Report 81-452.

4. Even though the juggling code did only half as many critical operations, its implementation overhead was twice that of the simpler reversal algorithm.

At the critical value of N, the machine ran out of real memory and had to page to disk. The reversal algorithm is well suited for paging: because of the locality of the reverse operation, it will read each disk page twice. On the other hand, the juggling algorithm is exactly "pessimal" for paging: it reads a page from disk, operates on a single element on the page, and returns to the page only after it has accessed every other page.

6. The signature of a name is its push-button encoding, so the signature of "LESK*M*" is "5375*6*". To find the false matches in a directory, we sign each name with its push-button encoding, sort by signature (and by name within equal signatures), and then sequentially read the sorted file to report any equal signatures with distinct names. To retrieve a name given its push-button encoding we use an intermediate file that contains the signatures and the other data. While we could sort that file and then look up a push-button encoding by binary search, in a real system we would probably use hashing or a disk file package.

7. To transpose the row-major matrix Vyssotsky prepended the column and row to each record, called the system tape sort to sort by column then row, and then removed the column and row numbers with a third program.

8. The *aha!* insight for this problem is that some K-element subset sums to at most T if and only if the subset consisting of the K smallest elements does. That subset can be found in time proportional to $N \log N$ by sorting the original set, or in time proportional to N by using a selection algorithm (see Solution 10.9). When Ullman assigned this as a class exercise, students designed algorithms with both running times mentioned above, as well as $O(N \log K)$, $O(NK)$, $O(N^2)$, and $O(N^K)$. Can you find natural algorithms to go with those running times?

10. Edison filled the shell with water and emptied it into a graduated cylinder. (As the hint may have reminded you, Archimedes also used water to compute volumes; in his day, *aha!* insights were celebrated by shouting *eureka!*)

   You can compute the center of gravity of a two-dimensional object (try it on a stiff book) by using your thumb, index finger, and middle finger as a tripod of support. As you close the tripod, the digit furthest from the center will support the least weight, have the least friction, and be the most likely to move; the tripod will therefore close on the center of gravity. Kee Dewdney discusses gadgets for analog computation in his "Computer Recreations" columns in the June 1984 and June 1985 *Scientific American*.

Solutions for Column 3

1 Each entry in a tax table contains three values: the lower bound for this bracket, the base tax, and the rate at which income over the lower bound is taxed. Including a final sentinel entry in the table with an "infinite" lower bound will make the sequential search easier to write and incidentally faster

(see Problem 8.5); one could also use a binary search. These techniques apply to any piecewise-linear functions.

3. This block letter "I"

```
XXXXXXXXX
XXXXXXXXX
XXXXXXXXX
    XXX
    XXX
    XXX
    XXX
    XXX
    XXX
XXXXXXXXX
XXXXXXXXX
XXXXXXXXX
```

might be encoded as

```
3 lines 9 X
6 lines 3 blank  3 X  3 blank
3 lines 9 X
```

or more compactly as

```
3 9 X
6 3 b 3 X 3 b
3 9 X
```

4. To find the number of days between two dates, compute the number of each day in its respective year, subtract the earlier from the later (perhaps borrowing from the year), and then add 365 times the difference in years plus one for each leap year. To find the day of the week for a given day, compute the number of days between the given day and a known Sunday, and then use modular arithmetic to convert that to a day of the week. To prepare a calendar for a month in a given year we need to know how many days there are in the month (take care to handle February correctly) and the day of the week on which the 1st falls.

5. Because the comparisons take place from the right to the left of the word, it will probably pay to store the words in reverse (right-to-left) order. Possible representations of a sequence of suffixes include a two-dimensional array of characters (which is usually wasteful), a single array of characters with the suffixes separated by a break character, and such a character array augmented with an array of pointers, one to each word.

8. "Programming Pearls" in the June 1985 *CACM* (pages 570-576) illustrates AWK's associative arrays. Most of the data structures discussed in Section 11.3 are suitable implementations of associative arrays in various contexts, but hashing is usually the method of choice.

Solutions for Column 4

1. To show that overflow does not occur we add the conditions $1 \leq L \leq N+1$ and $0 \leq U \leq N$ to the invariant; we can then bound $L+U$. The same conditions can be used to show that elements outside the array bounds are never accessed. We can formally define $MustBe(L,U)$ as $X[L-1]<T$ and $X[U+1]>T$ if we define the fictitious boundary elements $X[0]$ and $X[N+1]$ as in Section 8.3.

2. See Section 8.3.

5. For an introduction to this celebrated open problem of mathematics, see B. Hayes's "On the ups and downs of hailstone numbers" in the Computer Recreations column in the January 1984 *Scientific American*. For a more technical discussion, see "The $3x+1$ problem and its generalizations" by J. C. Lagarias, in the January 1985 *American Mathematical Monthly*.

6. The process terminates because each step decreases the number of beans in the can by one. It always removes either zero or two white beans from the coffee can, so it leaves invariant the parity (oddness or evenness) of the number of white beans. Thus the last remaining bean is white if and only if an odd number of white beans were in the can originally.

7. Because the line segments that form the rungs of the ladder are in increasing y-order, the two that bracket a given point can be found by binary search. The basic comparison in the search tells whether the point is below, on, or above a given line segment; how would you code that routine?

8. See Section 8.3.

10. "Programming Pearls" in the July 1985 *CACM* describes how I tested and debugged the binary search and selection algorithms.

Solutions for Column 5

1. The sequential program reads 10,000 blocks at 200 blocks/second, so it always requires 50 seconds. The on-line program reads R records in $R/20$ seconds, so when $R=100$ it takes five seconds; when $R=10,000$ it takes about eight minutes. The online program is faster when $R<1000$.

3. Using C on a VAX-11/750, double precision took about a third again as much time as single precision to compute the inner product of two vectors. Using BASIC on a personal computer, the times were indistinguishable. In both cases the systems did most of the computation in double precision, even though the results were truncated to single precision.

4. A laboratory system computed accurate images by working at the following levels: careful laboratory work to grow the culture, a 100-micron scanner to present the computer accurate images, and good but expensive image processing algorithms efficiently implemented on an array processor.

6. "Make it work first before you make it work fast" is usually good advice. However, it took Bill Wulf of Tartan Laboratories only a few minutes to convince me that the old truism isn't quite as true as I once thought. He used the case of a document production system that we both used. Although it was faster than its predecessor, at times it seemed excruciatingly slow: it took several hours to compile a book (although large documents could be compiled in pieces). Wulf's clincher went like this: "That program, like any other large system, today has ten known, but minor, bugs. Next month, it will have ten different known bugs. If you could choose between removing the ten current bugs or making the program run ten times faster, which would you pick?"

Solutions for Column 6

These solutions include guesses at constants that may be off by a factor of two from their correct values as this book went to press, but not much further.

1   6250 bytes per inch times a 2400 foot reel of tape times 0.5 for waste due to blocking gives 90 megabytes per reel of tape. 7000 bytes per second gives 25 megabytes per hour for the line. The bicyclist therefore has about three hours to transfer the data, which gives (say) a twenty-mile radius of superiority. The bicyclist has fifty times as long, or almost a week, to beat a 1200-baud line.

2. A large disk has about 200 megabytes, compared to 200 kilobytes for a 5.25 inch floppy disk. Flat out, my typing is about fifty words (or 300 bytes) per minute. A floppy therefore requires 700 minutes to fill (or about twelve hours), while a large disk requires a thousand times longer, or several years.

3. A terminal costs a couple of thousand dollars. A programmer (including many expenses beyond salary, unfortunately) costs about $100,000/yr, $2000/wk, $400/day, or $50/hr. Thus once a programmer has used the terminal for forty off-premise hours, the investment cost is recovered and the employer gets free work. (Page 630 of "Programming Pearls" in the July 1984 *CACM* contains two interesting letters discussing this problem. A programmer describes several ways to use a terminal at home and concludes that just a few hours of work at home could save forty hours of time on the job. A software manager lists a number of problems associated with home terminals, such as maintaining "health and safety standards around the terminal in compliance with the Walsh-Healey act".)

4. A one microsecond instruction takes one second, a 16 msec disk rotation (at 3600 rpm) takes 5 hrs, a 30 msec seek takes 10 hours, and the two seconds to type my name takes about a month.

5   In a second, a supercomputer can do a hundred million 64-bit floating point operations, a midicomputer can do one million 16-bit integer additions, a

microcomputer can execute half a million 8-bit instructions, and BASIC on a personal computer can execute one hundred instructions. The times stated in the problem work out to about the same amount of power for the first three machines, while poor BASIC is left way behind.

6. Ignoring slowdown due to queueing, 30 msec per disk operation gives 3 seconds per transaction or 1200 transactions per hour.

7. The cost of the change is $100 in machine time plus $400 in programmer time. The savings of 10 min/day is $16/day, which takes a month to pay for the investment. If the speedup were a factor of two, the savings of $80/day would pay for the speedup in a week.

9. Even I can enter digits at the rate of one per second, which translates to three records per minute or two hundred per hour. Having a data entry clerk re-key the data using familiar tools should therefore take less than two hours and cost less than fifty dollars. An automated solution would require substantial software on both PCs (I would search hard for packages before writing code myself), as well as the purchase of modems. Although the high-tech solution is clearly preferable for large volumes of data, the simple solution was superior for the problem at hand.

Solutions for Column 7

2. Algorithm 1 uses roughly $N^3/6$ calls to procedure *max*, Algorithm 2 uses roughly $N^2/2$ calls and Algorithm 4 uses roughly $2N$ calls. Algorithm 2b uses linear extra space for the cumulative array and Algorithm 3 uses logarithmic extra space for the stack; the other algorithms use only constant extra space. Algorithm 4 is online: it computes its answer in a single pass over the input, which is particularly useful for processing files on disk.

3. Replace the assignment $MaxSoFar:=0$ with $MaxSoFar:=-\infty$. If the use of $-\infty$ bothers you, $MaxSoFar:=X[1]$ does just as well; why?

4. Initialize the cumulative array *Cum* so that $Cum[I]=X[1]+ \ldots +X[I]$. The subvector $X[L..U]$ sums to zero if $Cum[L-1]=Cum[U]$. The subvector with the sum closest to zero is therefore found by locating the two closest elements in *Cum*, which can be done in $O(N \log N)$ time by sorting the array. That running time is within a constant factor of optimal because any algorithm for solving it can be used to solve the "Element Uniqueness" problem of determining whether an array contains duplicated elements (Dobkin and Lipton showed that the problem requires that much time in the worst case on a decision-tree model of computation).

5. The total cost between stations I and J on a linear turnpike is $Cum[J]-Cum[I-1]$, where *Cum* is a cumulative array, as above.

6. This solution uses yet another cumulative array. The loop

```
for I := L to U do
    X[I] := X[I]+V
```

is simulated by the assignments

```
Cum[U]   := Cum[U]+V
Cum[L-1] := Cum[L-1]-V
```

which symbolically add V to $X[1..U]$ and then subtract it from $X[1..L-1]$. After all such sums have been taken, we compute the array X by

```
for I := N-1 downto 1 do
    X[I] := X[I+1]+Cum[I]
```

This reduces the worst-case time for N sums from $O(N^2)$ to $O(N)$. This problem arose in gathering statistics on Appel's N-body program described in Section 5.1. Incorporating this solution reduced the run time of the statistics subroutine from four hours to twenty minutes; that speedup would have been inconsequential when the program took a year, but was important when it took just a day.

7. The maximum-sum subarray of an $M \times N$ array can be found in $O(M^2N)$ time by using the technique of Algorithm 2 in the dimension of length M and the technique of Algorithm 4 in the dimension of length N. The $N \times N$ problem can therefore be solved in N^3 time. This solution was discovered independently by more than a dozen readers; the names of most are listed on page 1092 of "Programming Pearls" in the November 1984 *CACM*. The best lower bound I know for this problem is proportional to N^2. Tightening the gap remained an open problem as this book went to press.

Solutions for Column 8

1. On a machine with eight-bit bytes a 256-byte table could represent the characters in eight (possibly overlapping) character classes. The Ith bit in byte J tells whether character J is in class I. Testing membership involves accessing an array element, ANDing with a bit pattern containing a single one, and comparing the result to zero.

2. Given N a power of two, we are to initialize $C[0..N-1]$ such that $C[I]$ is the number of one bits in the binary representation of I. We use the identity that $J < 2^K$ implies $C[J+2^K] = C[J]+1$; that is, turning on the Kth bit adds one to the count. For this reason each element in the right column is precisely one greater than the corresponding element in the left column.

```
C[0] = 0      C[8]  = 1
C[1] = 1      C[9]  = 2
C[2] = 1      C[10] = 2
C[3] = 2      C[11] = 3
C[4] = 1      C[12] = 2
C[5] = 2      C[13] = 3
C[6] = 2      C[14] = 3
C[7] = 3      C[15] = 4
```

This code therefore starts with a single-element table and repeatedly doubles its size by copying and incrementing; it runs in $O(N)$ time.

```
C[0] := 0
P := 1
while M < N do
    /* Invariant: C[0..M-1] is correct */
    for J := 0 to P-1 do
        C[M+J] := C[J]+1
    P := P+P
```

After this problem appeared in *CACM*, Jim de Boer of Scarborough, Ontario, and Rick Bonnett of Burlington, Vermont, found similar single-loop solutions. The key to de Boer's code is the fact that "the integer formed by removing the top one bit of J is $J-P$".

```
C[0] := 0
P := 1; PP := P+P
for J := 1 to N-1
    /* Invariant: P is a power of 2;
        PP = P+P; P <= J<= PP */
    if J = PP then
        P := PP; PP := P+P
    /* P is the greatest power of 2 <= J */
    C[J] := C[J-P]+1
```

The code runs in $O(N)$ time and works for all positive integers N.

3. If the binary search algorithms report that they found the search value T, then it is in fact in the table. When applied to unsorted tables, though, the algorithms may sometimes report that T is not present when it in fact is. In such cases the algorithms locate a pair of adjacent elements that would establish that T is not in the table were it sorted.

4. Brooks combined two representations for the table. The function got to within a few units of the true answer, and the single decimal digit stored in the array gave the difference.

6. "Programming Pearls" in the September 1984 *CACM* (pp. 870-871) sketches R. G. Dromey's derivation of a program that uses sentinels to compute the maximum element in an array. The resulting code is

```
I := 1
while I <= N do
    Max := X[I]; X[N+1] := Max; I := I+1
    while X[I] < Max do I := I+1
```

All the data structures mentioned can employ an additional sentinel node to remove a test from the inner loop of the search. Before a search starts it places the value being searched for in the sentinel node, which guarantees that the search will find its target. When the search succeeds a single comparison tells whether it found a "real" value or the value in the sentinel. This removes from the inner loop a test to determine whether the data structure is yet exhausted.

Linked lists have sentinel nodes at the very end; they must also store a pointer to that node (this is particularly convenient in a circularly linked list with a "dummy" node). Closed hash tables use a sentinel cell at the end of the array. Nil pointers in a standard binary search tree are replaced by pointers to a single sentinel node in the modified tree.

9. Replacing the function evaluations by several 72-element tables decreased the run time of the program on an IBM 7090 from half an hour to a minute. Because the evaluation of helicopter rotor blades required about three hundred runs of the program, those few hundred extra words of memory reduced a week of CPU time to several hours.

10. The UNIX system provides two profilers. The first reports the number of times each procedure was called, and also provides timing data. When run on the program on the next page, it produces

%time	cumsecs	#call	ms/call	name
35.2	0.26	233	1.11	_quicksort
31.8	0.49	7491	0.03	swap
13.6	0.59	1	100.04	_insort
8.0	0.65			mcount
6.8	0.70	1	50.02	_main
4.5	0.73			_rand

This output identifies the swap procedure as a good candidate for being rewritten in line.

A more detailed profiler writes the entire program text, together with numbers in the left column that count how often each statement was executed. Beware of a few mistakes near closing brackets, a problem with this particular profiler.

```
1          #include <stdio.h>
1          int n, x[1001];
1
1          main()
1          {   int i;
1              n = 1000;
1              for (i = 1; i <= n; i++) x[i] = rand();
1              quicksort(1, n); insort();
1              for (i = 1; i < n; i++)
999                if (x[i] > x[i+1])
0                     printf("Bug in quicksort");
7491       }
7491
7491       swap(px, py)
7491       int *px, *py;
7491       {   int t;
1              t = *px; *px = *py; *py = t;
1          }
1
1          insort()
1          {   int i, j;
1              for (i = 2; i <= n; i++) {
999                j = i;
3115               while (j > 1 && x[j] < x[j-1]) {
2116                   swap(&x[j], &x[j-1]);
2116                   j--;
999                }
233            }
233        }
233
233        quicksort(l, u)
233        int l, u;
233        {   int i, m;
233            if (u-l > 15) {
116                swap(&x[l], &x[l+(u-l+1)*rand()/32768]);
116                m = l;
116                for (i = l+1; i <= u; i++)
9288                   if (x[i] < x[l])
5143                       swap(&x[++m], &x[i]);
9288               swap(&x[l], &x[m]);
116                quicksort(l, m-1);
116                quicksort(m+1, u);
116        }
```

This program is discussed in Section 10.2. Note that the Insertion Sort's loop sifts each element down only 2.1 positions, on the average. What other counts tell interesting tales?

11. Horner's method evaluates the polynomial by

```
Y := A[N]
for I := N-1 downto 0 do
    Y := X*Y + A[I]
```

It uses N multiplications, and is usually twice as fast as the previous code.

Solutions for Column 9

1. Every high-level language instruction that accessed one of the packed fields compiled into many machine instructions; accessing an unpacked field required fewer instructions. By unpacking the records, Feldman slightly increased data space but greatly reduced code space and run time.

2. Several readers suggested storing $(x, y, PointIdentifier)$ triples sorted by y within x; binary search can then be used to look up a given (x,y) pair. The data structure described in the text is easiest to build if the input has been sorted by x values (and within x by y, as above). The structure described in the text could be searched more quickly by performing a binary search in the Row array between values $FirstInCol[I]$ and $FirstInCol[I+1]-1$. Note that those y values appear in increasing order and that the binary search must correctly handle the case of searching an empty subarray. The space for the structure could be reduced to 2000 16-bit words by "key indexing": the Ith element of an array contains two one-byte fields that give the x and y positions of point I.

3. Almanacs store tables of distances between cities as triangular arrays, which reduces their space by a factor of two. Mathematical tables sometimes store only the least significant digits of functions, and give the most significant digits just once, say, for each row of values. Television schedules save space by only stating when shows start (as opposed to listing all shows that are on at any given thirty-minute interval). Classified advertisements in newspapers save space by abbreviated encodings for items such as houses and cars; this highly compressed data is typical of "personals" columns.

> Shy 34yo SWM, MD, 5'9" 155lbs ints
> incl clas/flk mus, rding, joggng, movies
> sks pretty slender intel SWF for long-
> term rel ph/ph plse.

4. The sequence can be shortened by encoding runs of equal characters. We will use the three numbers "0, n, x" to denote n occurrences of the number x; a single zero is encoded as "0, 1, 0". The sequence in the problem is then compressed to

$$0, 38, 128, 152, 166, 172, 153, 164, 0, 19, 128$$

which replaces 62 bytes by 11 bytes.

5. The original file required 300 kilobytes of disk memory. Compressing two digits into one byte reduced that to 150 kilobytes but increased the time to read the file. Replacing the expensive *div* and *mod* operations with a table lookup cost 200 bytes of primary memory but reduced the read time almost to its original cost. Thus 200 bytes of primary memory bought 150 kilobytes of disk. Other encodings, such as representing A and B by $16 \times A + B$, might have given comparable speed without using the table, and offer other advantages as well (see the footnote in Section 9.2).

Solutions for Column 10

1. Sorting to find the minimum or maximum of N floating point numbers is usually overkill. Solution 9 shows how the median can be found more quickly without sorting, but sorting might be easier on some systems. Sorting is usually just right for finding the mode. While the obvious code for finding the mean takes time proportional to N, an approach that first sorts might be able to accomplish the job with greater numerical accuracy; see Problem 12.3.b.

2. The given code fails when the system provides array bounds checking and both conjuncts are evaluated, even though the first is false. A similar situation arises in the Insertion Sort in Section 10.1 when $J = 1$. Failure can be avoided in a number of ways, such as using a conditional AND operator, declaring $X[0]$ (and possibly using it as a sentinel), placing the minimum value in $X[1]$ before calling the main sort, or using a boolean variable.

3. If all elements are equal, the Quicksort in the column removes only one element at each of N recursive calls. Sedgewick's code has this invariant.

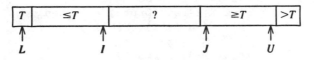

By "wasting" swaps on equal elements, it exactly halves a subarray of duplicate keys.

4. Bob Sedgewick observed that Lomuto's partitioning scheme can be modified to work from right to left by using the following invariant:

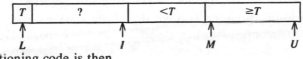

The partitioning code is then

```
M := U+1
for I := U downto L do
    if X[I] >= T then
        M := M-1
        Swap(X[M], X[I])
```

Upon termination we know that $X[M]=T$, so we can recur with parameters $(L,M-1)$ and $(M+1,U)$; no additional *Swap* is needed. Sedgewick also used $X[L]$ as a sentinel to remove one test from the inner loop

```
M := U+1
I := U+1
repeat
    repeat I := I-1 until X[I] >= T
    M := M-1
    Swap(X[M], X[I])
until I = L
```

5. See Sedgewick's paper cited in Section 10.5.

6. McIlroy's program runs in time proportional to the amount of data to be sorted, which is optimal in the worst case. It assumes that each record in $X[1..N]$ has an integer *Length* and a pointer to the array $Bit[1..Length]$.

```
procedure Sort(L, U, Depth)
    if L < U then
        for I := L to U do
            if X[I].Length < Depth then
                Swap(X[I], X[L])
                L := L+1
        M := L
        for I := L to U do
            if X[I].Bit[Depth] = 0 then
                Swap(X[I], X[M])
                M := M+1
        Sort(L, M-1, Depth+1)
        Sort(M, U, Depth+1)
```

The procedure is originally called by *Sort*(1,N, 1). This program assigns values to parameters and to variables defining **for** loops; although that is fine in many languages, it is illegal in others (such as Pascal). The linear running time depends strongly on the fact that the *Swap* operation moves pointers to the bit strings and not the bit strings themselves.

8. The answer to this question is quite dependent on your particular system. For a thorough but somewhat dated answer, see page 170 of W. A. Martin's article "Sorting" in *Computing Surveys 3*, 4, December 1971.

9. This algorithm is due to C. A. R. Hoare; it is discussed in Programming Pearls in the November 1985 *Communications of the ACM*.

```
procedure Select(L, U, K)
      pre L <= K <= U
      post X[L..K-1] <= X[K] <= X[K+1..U]
  if L < U then
      Swap(X[L], X[RandInt(L,U)])
      T := X[L]
      M := L
      for I := L+1 to U do
          /* Invariant: X[L+1..M] < T
              and X[M+1..I-1] >= T */
          if X[I] < T then
              M := M+1
              Swap(X[M], X[I])
      Swap(X[L], X[M])
      /* X[L..M-1] <= X[M] <= X[M+1..U] */
      if      M < K then Select(M+1, U, K)
      else if M > K then Select(L, M-1, K)
```

The code can be improved in many ways. The partitioning code in Problem 10.3, for instance, avoids an expensive worst case. Because the recursion is the last action of the procedure, it can be transformed into a while loop.

```
procedure Select(K)
      post X[1..K-1] <= X[K] <= X[K+1..N]
  L := 1; U := N
  while L < U do
      /* Invariant: X[1..L-1] <= X[L..U] <= X[U+1..N] */
      ... loop body here ...
      /* Invariant and X[L..M-1] <= X[M] <= X[M+1..U] */
      if M <= K then L := M+1
      if M >= K then U := M-1
```

In Problem 5.2.2-32 of *Sorting and Searching*, Knuth shows that the program uses an average of $3.4N$ comparisons to find the median of N elements; the probabilistic argument is similar in spirit to the worst-case argument in Solution 2.A. For intuition about the performance, I gathered this data with a 16-line AWK program that generated random data, ran the algorithm, and collected statistics.

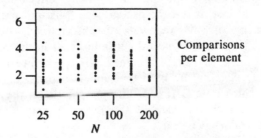

Comparisons per element

Only rarely does the program require more than $4N$ comparisons to find the median of an *N*-element array. (Compare this "flat" data to the rising trend in the second graph in the next solution.)

10. The top graph plots the run time of Quicksort 2 as a function of the size of the input array, *N*. The one hundred *N* values are uniformly spaced along the logarithmic scale. The small times are discrete because my system measures run time in sixtieths of a second. That graph shows that run time is strongly correlated to input size, but provides little insight beyond that.

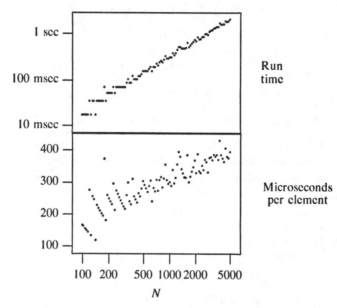

The y-scale in the bottom graph is the run time per array element in microseconds (that is, the total time divided by *N*). This graph displays the wide variation in run time due to the randomizing *Swap*. The straightness of the data (past 500, at least) indicates that the run time per element grows logarithmically, which implies that the overall run time of Quicksort is $O(N \log N)$. Most algorithms texts give a mathematical proof of this fact.

12. The circulation department at *Scientific American* receives a large volume of mail. (Back-of-the-envelope quiz: how many letters does the magazine receive per day?) Most of the correspondence falls into half a dozen major categories: payments of bills, renewals of subscriptions, responses to direct mail promotions, responses to postal cards inserted in the magazine, and so forth. The mail must be sorted into these groups before it is processed by data entry clerks. Sorting the mail by hand is expensive, so the magazine has the United States Post Office do the job for them: they use a different post office box number for each of the major categories (each box costs about a hundred dollars per year).

Solutions for Column 11

1. To select M integers from the range $1..N$, choose the number I at random in the range, and then report the numbers I, $I+1$, ..., $I+M-1$, possibly wrapping around to 1. This method chooses each integer with probability M/N, but is strongly biased towards certain subsets.

2. When fewer than $N/2$ integers have been selected so far, the probability that a randomly chosen integer is unselected is greater than $1/2$. That the average number of draws to get an unselected integer is less than 2 follows from the logic that one must toss a coin twice, on the average, to get heads.

3. Let's view the set S in Program 2 as a collection of N initially empty urns. Each call to `RandInt` selects an urn into which we throw a ball; if it was previously occupied, the *Member* test is true. The number of balls required to ensure that each urn contains at least one ball is known to statisticians as the "Coupon Collector's Problem" (how many baseball cards must I collect to make sure I have all N?); the answer is roughly $N \ln N$. The algorithm makes M tests when all the balls go into different urns; determining when there are likely to be two balls in one urn is the "Birthday Paradox" (in any group of 23 or more people, two are likely to share a birthday). In general, two balls are likely to share one of N urns if there are $O(\sqrt{N})$ balls.

6. To print the values in increasing order one can place the print statement after the recursive call, or print $N+1-I$ rather than I.

7. To print distinct integers in random order, print each one as it is first generated; also see the solution to Problem 1.4. To print duplicate integers in sorted order, remove the test of whether the integer is already in the set. To print duplicate integers in random order, use the trivial program

```
for I := 1 to M do
    print RandInt(1,N)
```

8. I gave this problem, exactly as stated, on a take-home examination in a course on "Applied Algorithm Design". Students who described methods that could compute the answer in just a few minutes of CPU time received zero points. The response "I'd talk to my statistics professor" was worth half credit, and a perfect answer went like this:

> The numbers $4..10$ have no impact on the game, so they can be ignored. The card wins if 1 and 2 are chosen (in either order) before 3. This happens when 3 is chosen last, which occurs one time out of three. The probability that a random sequence wins is therefore precisely $1/3$.

Don't be misled by problem statements; you don't have to use the CPU time just because it's available!

Solutions for Column 12

1. The modified *SiftDown* is

```
procedure SiftDown(L,U)
        pre    MaxHeap(L+1,U)
        post   MaxHeap(L,U)
    I := L
    loop
        /* Invariant: MaxHeap(L,U) except perhaps
            between I and its (0, 1 or 2) children */
        C := 2*I
        if C > U then break
        if C+1 <= U and X[C+1] > X[C] then C := C+1
        /* C is the greatest child of I */
        if X[I] >= X[C] then break
        Swap(X[C], X[I])
        I := C
```

The and in the second if statement must be conditional. The procedure's run time is $O(\log U - \log L)$. This code builds a heap in $O(N)$ time

```
for I := N-1 downto 1 do
    /* Invariant: MaxHeap(I+1, N) */
    SiftDown(I, N)
    /* MaxHeap(I, N) */
```

Because *MaxHeap*(L,N) is true for all integers $L>N/2$, the bound $N-1$ in the for loop can be changed to $int(N/2)$.

2. Using the code in Solution 1, the Heapsort is

```
for I := int(N/2) downto 1 do
    SiftDown(I, N)
for I := N downto 2 do
    Swap(X[1], X[I])
    SiftDown(1, I-1)
```

Its running time remains $O(N \log N)$, but with a smaller constant than in the original Heapsort. *SiftDown* can be made faster by moving the *Swap* assignments to and from the temporary variable *T* out of its loop. The *SiftUp* procedure can be made faster by moving code out of loops and by placing a sentinel element in $X[0]$ to remove the test if I=1.

3. Heaps replace a $O(N)$ step by a $O(\log N)$ step in all the problems.

   a. The iterative step in building a Huffman code selects the two smallest nodes in the set and merges them into a new node; this is implemented by two *ExtractMins* followed by an *Insert*. If the input frequencies are presented in sorted order, then the Huffman code can be computed in linear time; the details are left as an exercise.

   b. A simple algorithm to sum floating point numbers might lose accuracy by adding very small numbers to large numbers. A superior algorithm always adds the two smallest numbers in the set, and is isomorphic to the Huffman code algorithm mentioned above.

c. A 1000-element heap (minimum at top) represents the 1000 largest numbers seen so far.

d. A heap can be used to merge sorted files by representing the next element in each file; the iterative step selects the smallest element from the heap and inserts its successor into the heap. The next element to be output from N files can be chosen in $O(\log N)$ time. (Linderman's paper cited in Section 10.5 describes how this algorithm increased the run time of a real system sort; he reduced the time by using a binary search.)

4. A heap-like structure is placed over the sequence of bins; each node in the heap tells the amount of space left in the least full bin among its descendants. When deciding where to place a new weight, the search goes left if it can (i.e., the least full bin to the left has enough space to hold it) and right if it must; that requires time proportional to the heap's depth of $O(\log N)$. After the weight is inserted, the path is traversed up to fix the weights in the heap. David Johnson, Tom Leighton, Cathy McGeoch and I used this algorithm to conduct experiments on the performance of bin packing; we were able to solve problems of size $N - 100,000$ in one minute, while previous programs that used sequential search required that long for $N = 1000$.

5. The common implementation of a sequential file on disk has block I point to block $I+1$. McCreight observed that if node I also points to node $2I$, then an arbitrary node N can be found in at most $1 + \log_2 N$ accesses. The following recursive program prints the access path.

```
function Path(N)
        pre    integer N >= 0
        post   Path to N is printed
    if N = 0 then
        print "Start at 0"
      else if Even(N) then
        Path(N/2)
        print "Double to ", N
      else
        Path(N-1)
        print "Increment to ", N
```

Notice that it is isomorphic to the program for computing X^N in $O(\log N)$ steps given in Problem 4.9.

6. The modified binary search begins with $I=1$, and at each iteration sets I to either $2I$ or $2I+1$. $X[1]$ contains the median element, $X[2]$ contains the first quartile, $X[3]$ the third quartile, and so on. S. R. Mahaney of Bell Labs and J. I. Munro of the University of Waterloo found a routine to put

an N-element sorted array into "Heapsearch" order in $O(N)$ time and $O(1)$ extra space. As a precursor to their method, consider copying a sorted array A of size $2^K - 1$ into a "Heapsearch" array B: the odd elements of A go, in order, into the last half of the elements of B, elements congruent to 2 modulo 4 go into B's second quarter, and so on.

10. I implemented heap-based priority queues in Stroustrup's *C++ Programming Language* (the book was published by Addison-Wesley in 1986). A member of the class of priority queues is defined to have the following attributes.

```
class priqueue {
    int n, maxsize;
    float *x;
    void swap(int, int);
    int heap(int, int);
public:
    priqueue(int);
    void insert(float);
    float extractmin();
};
```

Public parts are available to users of the class, while the private parts (variables and routines) are available only to the implementer. In this case, users see only the *insert* and *extractmin* routines, and (implicitly) the following routine that creates an element of the class. (The name of the "creator" procedure is the class name.)

```
priqueue::priqueue(int m)
{   if (m < 1) error("illegal size");
    maxsize = m;
    x = new float[maxsize+1];
    n = 0;
}
```

The routine checks the maximum size of the priority queue, stores it in *maxsize*, allocates a new array, and initializes *n*. The array is declared of size *maxsize* + 1 because C++ arrays are zero-based, while heaps use 1-based arrays. My implementation uses an ASSERT macro to check the invariant of the data structure.

```
#define ASSERT(e) if (!(e)) error("assertion failed")
```

Macros in C++ are the same as in C. The priority queue class has a private function that is true (returns one) if the array has the heap property and is false otherwise.

```
int priqueue::heap(int 1, int u)
{   for (int i = 2*1; i <= u; i++)
        if (x[i/2] > x[i]) return 0;
    return 1;
}
```

I used it to test the code, but this routine is so expensive that production versions should define the ASSERT macro to be null to avoid evaluation of *heap*.

This routine inserts *t* into the priority queue. It tests the invariant of the data structure on entry and exit.

```
void priqueue::insert(float t)
{   ASSERT(heap(1,n));
    if (++n > maxsize) error("too many elements");
    x[n] = t;
    int i = n;
    for (;;) { /* invariant: heap(1,n) except
              perhaps between i and its parent */
        if (i == 1) break;
        int p = i/2;
        if (x[p] < x[i]) break;
        swap(p, i);
        i = p;
    }
    ASSERT(heap(1, n));
}
```

The for statement starts a loop that is terminated by a break statement, and *swap* is a private routine that exchanges the named elements of the array *x*. The *swap* and *extractmin* routines are similarly defined. The resulting class is used in this sample program that fills array *a* with integers and then sorts them.

```
main()
{   /* declare and initialize array */
    int n = 10; float a[n];
    for (int i = 0; i < n; i++) a[i] = n-i;

    /* sort using priority queues */
    priqueue q(n);
    for (i = 0; i < n; i++) q.insert(a[i]);
    for (i = 0; i < n; i++) a[i] = q.extractmin();
}
```

The line following the second comment declares *q* to be of type priority queue with maximum size *n*; it is similar to the array declaration float a[n] in the third line. The two subsequent lines apply the operations to the object *q*. The class might also be used in declarations like

```
priqueue events(30);
priqueue times(maxtimes);
```

The language allocates storage for the various priority queues, and associates the variables *n* and *x* with the proper objects. The user may now think of priority queues as a new primitive type, just like integers or arrays.

Solutions for Column 13

1. "Statistical text processing" by McMahon, Cherry and Morris appeared in the *Bell System Technical Journal 57*, 6, part 2 (July-August 1978, pp. 2137-2154). It describes tools for gathering statistics and the result of using the tools.

2. The graph on the left shows the VAX/11-750 run time of `spell` on the thirteen columns in this book as a function of the total number of words; the column number is plotted. I gathered the data using the UNIX system's word count program `wc`.

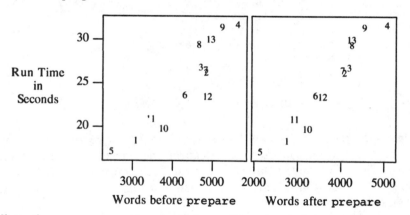

Words before `prepare`   Words after `prepare`

When the curve was not as straight as I expected, I immediately realized the problem: Column 12, for instance, runs quickly because it includes many pictures never seen by `spell`. The graph on the right therefore counts the words that remain after the `prepare` program (in this case, the UNIX system's `deroff`) removes the formatting commands; it gives a more accurate predictor of run time.

3. See "Experience with a space efficient way to store a dictionary" by R. Nix (in the May 1981 *CACM*) and "Reducing dictionary size by using a hashing technique" by D. J. Dodds (in the June 1982 *CACM*).

4. One approach sorts the words in the document and scans for near misses (such as *programmer* and *programer*); it might pay to do this with the words both forwards and backwards (to catch *pregrammer*). The paper cited in Solution 1 describes a program that reads a document, counts the frequency

of all letter pairs and triples, and then reports words with strange patterns (such as the double-x in *REXX*).

5. A spelling suggester might apply certain operations to the input word (such as transposing two adjacent letters or adding or deleting a single letter) and report all permutations that are in the dictionary. For an interactive approach appropriate for small dictionaries, see "Spelling correction in user interfaces" by Durham, Lamb and Saxe in the October 1983 *CACM*. A different approach might use the Soundex method mentioned in Section 2.5.

7. McIlroy's paper cited in Section 13.6 describes a "British" option that handles words like *centre*, *favour*, *realise*, and *speciality*.

8. L. Cherry's "Writing tools" appeared in *IEEE Transactions on Communications COM-30*, 1 (January 1982, pp. 100-104). It describes a host of programs for finding offenses such as wordy phrases, bad diction, punctuation errors, and split infinitives.

INDEX

For information on particular algorithms or data structures, consult also the Catalog of Algorithms (the Appendix on pages 155 through 158).

Nijenhuis, A. 124
Nixon, R. M. 144
numbers, prime 94
numbers, random 111, 118
numerical analysis 47, 79, 91, 94, 135, 176

Olympic games 59
Oppenheimer, R. 67
OR, conditional 86
overlaying data structures 98, 132

packing, bin 183
page4-5 3
paper bags 119
Parnas, D. L. 32
partitioning routines 109-111, 115, 116,
    177-179
Pascal 8, 10, 53, 62, 88, 100, 149, 178
Penzias, A. A. vi
performance bugs 62, 64, 84, 112, 143, 174,
    183
performance requirements 4, 13, 49, 52, 54,
    59, 63, 64, 84, 90, 143
personal computers 64, 66, 75, 97, 98, 99,
    103, 117, 169, 170
Peterson, J. J. 149
physics 51, 67
pictures 28, 32, 81, 99, 102
piecewise-linear functions 168
pigeons 164
Pike, R. 66
Pinkham, R. 68
pipelines 19, 20, 139
Plauger, P. J. v, 3, 4, 10, 13, 15, 29, 116,
    139
pointers 97, 102, 162, 168, 178
political redistricting 4
Polya, G. 31, 60, 123
Post Office 180
postconditions 43
Potter, H. 68
precincts 4, 117
precomputed results, store 77, 78, 82, 83, 89,
    101, 165
preconditions 43
prime numbers 94
primitives 13-15, 17
priority queues 130-132, 135, 184
probability 124
problem definition 3, 6, 17, 19, 31, 53, 66,
    76, 78, 90, 94, 102, 117, 119, 122, 141,
    144, 164, 180, 181
problem-solving process 17
problems, geometric 80, 83
procedures, inline 113

process, design 7, 30, 49, 55, 59, 62, **64, 76-**
    77, 93, 99, 122, 147, 150, 151
profilers 52, 65, 81, 88, 91, 102, 174, **175**
program verification 35-48, 74, 85-88, 110-
    112, 125-134, 166, 173, 177, 179, 182
program verification system 48
programmer time 3, 6, 30, 48, 53, 56, 63, **66,**
    81, 82, 84, 92, 96, 100, 108, 115, 123,
    139-140
programming languages *see* AWK, BASIC,
    C, C++, COBOL, FORTRAN, MIX,
    Pascal, Ratfor, SNOBOL
programming, bottom-up 39, 99, **125**
programming, dynamic 102
programming, top-down 37, 39, **99**
programs, binary search 38, 85-88
programs, generator 94
programs, isomorphic 166, 183
programs, needlessly big 3, 23-32, 99, **101,**
    109, 123, 148, 152, 181
programs, reliable 7, 31, 56, 63
programs, robust 7, 8, 47, 56, 93
programs, secure 7, 48, 55, 56
programs, subtle 14, 35, 73, 74, 78, 85-88,
    98, 108, 110, 112, 118, 129-130, 144-146,
    166, 173, 176, 178
programs, traveling salesman 98
prototypes 123, 140, 147, 149
pseudocode 36
Public, J. Q. 26
punched cards 12, 13, 24
Purcell, E. 67
purchase orders 53

queues, priority 130-132, 135, 184
quick tests 60-61
Quicksort 4, 109-116, 161, 175

radix sort 178
random numbers 111, 118
random samples 117
random sets 8, 117-124, 163, 179
randomizing algorithms 13, 111, 112
Ratfor 3, 4
recompute answers 94
records, variable-length 98
recurrence relations 32, 73, 79
recursion 14, 45, 46, 72, 109, 112, 124, **165,**
    178, 179
Reddy, D. R. 57
redistricting, political 4
Reingold, E. M. 13, 83, 165
relations, equivalence 16
reliable programs 7, 31, 56, 63
requirements, performance 4, 13, 49, 52, **54,**
    59, 63, 64, 84, 90, 143